WATER PLANNING FOR FOOD PRODUCTION IN DEVELOPING COUNTRIES

Phillip Z. Kirpich

University Press of America,® Inc.
Lanham • New York • Oxford

Copyright © 1999 by
University Press of America,® Inc.
4720 Boston Way
Lanham, Maryland 20706

12 Hid's Copse Rd.
Cumnor Hill, Oxford OX2 9JJ

Library of Congress Cataloging-in-Publication Data

Kirpich, Phillip Z.
Water planning for food production in developing countries / Phillip
Z. Kirpich.
p.   cm.
Includes bibliographical references.
1. Water—supply, Agricultural—Developing countries. I. title.
S494.5.W3K57 1999   631.7'09172'4—dc21   99—32459 CIP

ISBN 0-7618-1448-5 (cloth: alk. ppr.)

This book is dedicated to my wife

Billie Kirpich

Contents

List of Figures

Preface

Although global food production is higher than it has ever been, it must be greatly increased in order to keep pace with the global population, which is continuing to grow rapidly in the developing countries. A major part of this growing population suffers from extreme poverty, causing cutting and burning of forests, cultivation of steep unsuitable land and other environmental damage. This population is also desperate for higher living standards, including food of adequate quality, much of it derived from animal sources. If the future need for more and better quality food is not met, the developed countries will also suffer, as a result of the ensuing environmental damage and social and political instability.

This book has four aims. The first is to increase awareness of the general public—and of their political leaders—of the need to improve the management of water. This need is urgent especially in the developing countries.

- Most of the required increases in quantity and quality of food in many key regions of the world will have to come from irrigated agriculture, and water in these regions is becoming scarce.
- Concurrently, there is increased competition for water among agricultural, industrial, urban, hydroelectric, river transport, recreation and environmental uses.
- The output of irrigated agriculture is also being threatened by depletion of aquifers, by degradation of water quality, and by lack of systematic drainage causing rising watertables and salinization.
- Agriculture in humid zones also suffers from lack of systematic drainage, although some drainage schemes, as in the Everglades of South Florida, have gone too far in eliminating wetlands that serve to conserve floodwaters and wildlife habitats.

A second aim is to describe the *complexity of water management*. Water has multiple uses and is "managed" by a multiplicity of agencies, even within a single country. In order for water management to succeed, particularly in developing countries, its *holistic* nature has to be understood, which means that social, environmental, economic, institutional and people-management elements have to be factored in. All of these elements are in turn greatly affected by government policies on matters such as farm subsidies and taxes, land tenure systems, import and export taxes, support of credit schemes for small farmers, rural infrastructure (such as domestic water supply and roads) and the extent of autonomy granted to local government. Chapter 2 presents an amplified description of the term "water management" as applied to developing countries.

A third aim is to describe *lessons learned* with respect to the carrying out of water management in developing countries. Thirty actual cases in 25 countries are described in Chapters 3 to 8, based on the author's experience. Many of these cases are updated based on data from other sources. Each chapter contains many references to selected literature published during the past several decades.

Finally, the fourth aim is to consider *best practices* to deal with water management in developing countries. Chapter 9 starts with a global perspective, followed by check lists suitable for use by water-resource planners at regional and project levels. This in turn is followed by a discussion of the key roles played by international agencies that provide financing as well as advice to developing countries. The chapter ends by describing what these countries themselves must do to improve water management as a key factor to achieve increased food production.

The book deals little with *design* of water-control structures but rather with what many practitioners, the author included, consider seriously lacking at the present time: effective water-resource *policies, institutions and management*. Matters which in the author's opinion merit priority are described including suggested steps to gain support of the general public and their political leaders. No doubt other practitioners will have similar suggestions to offer.

Acknowledgements

Colleagues, with almost all of whom I have had long association, provided important guidance, suggestions and assistance. Among them were Thomas Naff, Professor, Asian and Middle East Studies, University of Pennsylvania; Gabriel J. Tibor, Division Chief for irrigation in India, World Bank (retired); Harald D. Frederiksen, Irrigation Engineer, World Bank (retired); Theodore M. Schad, former Executive Director, National Water Commission; Montague Yudelman, Director for Agriculture, World Bank (retired); Otto J. Helweg, Dean, College of Engineering and Architecture, North Dakota State University; and Marvin E. Jensen, former President, International Commission on Irrigation and Drainage.

Professor Robert Giegengack, Chair, Department of Earth and Environmental Science, University of Pennsylvania, and one of his graduate students, Jennifer Smith, provided invaluable support in preparation of the maps.

My wife, Billie, read the text, provided comments on issues that concerned her, such as mass poverty and safeguarding the environment, and endured loneliness while I labored at the word processor.

Chapter 1

WORLD POPULATION AND AGRICULTURAL PRODUCTION

The world population in mid-1997 was about 6 billion. Projections for the year 2050 by the United Nations range from 7.7 billion to 11.2 billion.[1] The figure actually reached will depend primarily on the birth rate in the developing countries. According to the UN's medium projection, the 2050 population will be 9.4 billion, which is not far from that used by the World Bank in 1994.[2] From Fig. 1-1, note that almost all of the increase will be in the *developing countries*.

The term "developing countries" is interchangeable with "lesser developed countries," also referred to as "LDCs." In 1995, when the countries of the world numbered 133, the World Bank placed them into four categories according to Gross National Product (GNP) per capita. In 1995 these were: Low, $80 to 750; Lower Middle, 760 to 3,020; Upper Middle, 3,050 to 9,500; and high, over 9,500.[3] (There were no countries in the range 7,500 to 12,000. The GNP per capita of the U.S. in 1995 was $26,980.) If developing countries are designated as those in the two lowest categories, in 1995 there were 90 such countries, with GNP per capita ranging from about $80 to $3,020, and their population was about 4.8 billion or 84 percent of the world population of 5.7 billion.

World Food: Future Demand and Supply

Leading authorities, including those listed in the references,[4] have
described probable future *trends* with respect to the demand and supply

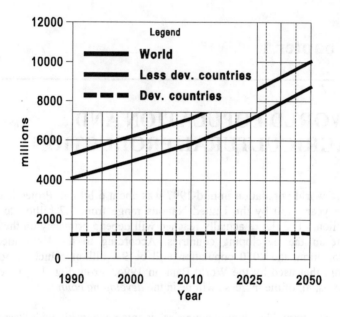

Figure 1-1. World Population. Source: World Bank (IIMI Review
1994).[2]

of food. Their general consensus is that there is no immediate threat of
a *global* food shortage, but that it is urgent to institute planning to avoid
shortages in several key *regions,* all of which are in the developing
countries. These include the Middle East and North Africa, Sub-
Saharan Africa, India, Pakistan, China, Mexico and Brazil.

There are a few economists that take a more optimistic point of
view, claiming that the authorities forming the consensus are overly
pessimistic *Neo-Malthusians.* (Malthus, early 19th century English
economist, mistakenly foretold disaster resulting from the burgeoning
world population.) These economists foresee more *Green Revolutions,*

like the one that, based on improved seeds and irrigation, brought sharply higher yields of grain in the 1960s and 1970s; and they appear confident that future breakthroughs in biotechnology will bring further increases in yields.[5]

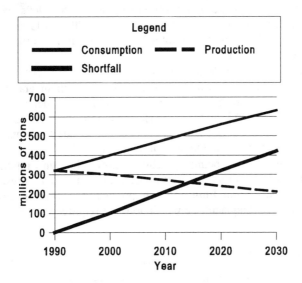

Figure 1-2. Grains in China: Production, Consumption and Shortfall. Source: USDA, Census Bureau[6]

The concerns of the consensus, which appear to the author to be well founded, may be summarized as follows:

• Population increases plus the desire for improved diets (more livestock products) will greatly raise the global demand for grains. A case in point is China, whose grain production is presently reaching limits and is expected to decline substantially in coming decades (Fig. 1-2). Concurrently, China's consumption of grains is likely to almost double in the next 40years as the population rises and as people demand higher living standards including more meat, much of it derived from grain. (World consumption of meat increased from 44 million metric tons in 1950 to 200 million metric tons in 1995.) According to one forecaster,[6] China's shortfall in grain may reach 210 million tons by 2010 and 420 million tons by 2030; other analysts[7] are hopeful that China's grain imports may not reach quite that high. Similar shortfalls are likely for India.

- The global output of grain rose greatly during the 1960s and 1970s but there has been little or no rise since 1990. World grain prices soared in 1995 and may double by 2010 according to the Japanese Ministry of Agriculture.[8]
- Trends in recent decades have been unfavorable with respect to world grain production. There has been a drop in grainland per person, caused by growing urbanization and deterioration of agricultural land, and a decrease since 1990 in fertilizer use, the latter due to the fact that the increased yield due to its application has become too small to be profitable (Fig. 1-3).[6]
- Curtailment is being practiced now through international agreement in order to prevent deterioration and to preserve, at least, the natural limits of fish production. There is scope for expansion of aquaculture which however requires scarce and costly grain.

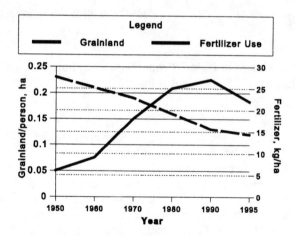

Fig. 1-3. World Fertilizer Use and Grainland per Person. Source: USDA, FAO[6]

- Production from ocean fisheries has reached natural limits. Water

Overpumping of several major aquifers is occuring, among them those of the Punjab of India and Pakistan, North China, Northwest Mexico and the Ogallala in the United States. The rapid urbanization taking place in most developing countries will increase competition for scarce water and thereby further reduce its availability for agriculture.

- Other water-related negative effects are being caused by salinization, pollution, soil erosion and flooding.
- Other than water, serious impediments to agricultural production in the developing countries are resulting from fragmentation of landholdings, poor land management, and bad macro-economic policies with respect to land tenure, land taxation, subsidies, and export and import taxes.
- Global warming, caused by burning of fossil fuels, could result in climatic changes that would affect agricultural production, the availability of water and the frequency and duration of floods. Although the magnitude of these effects are as yet unknown, most scientists feel that advanced long-range planning is needed for efficient energy use, water conservation and agricultural sustainability so as to cope with possible climate-induced changes.[9]

The Crucial Importance of Irrigated Agriculture

Arable land on the planet, totaling about 1.5 billion hectares (ha), is almost fully utilized. The one-sixth that is in the irrigated sector, about 250 million ha, will have to be the main supplier of the increased demand, but its output will have to be greatly increased. That means squeezing more crop yield from the *available water.*

Except for the miniscule amount of fresh water derived from the seas through desalination, the volume of fresh water available for human use equals the runoff on the land from natural rainfall. Hydrologists have made a sufficiently reliable estimate of the average annual global rainfall and of the runoff on land, termed *renewable fresh water supply on land* ($RFWS_{LAND}$), estimated at 40,000 cubic kilometers (km^3) annually. Much land, as in the Amazon rainforest, is inaccessible. Hydrologists have estimated the *accessible runoff* (AR) to be about 12,500 km^3. Of the latter, humanity now uses 54 percent.[10]

In examining the question of available water, one must of course consider not only the global but also the regional amounts, bearing in

In examining the question of available water, one must of course consider not only the global but also the regional amounts, bearing in mind that water can only in exceptional cases be transported economically more than a few hundred kilometers. The key regions mentioned earlier as being subject to risk of food shortage are also those with growing water shortages. These regions will need detailed studies by hydrologists for determination of the available water in each case. Concurrently, economic studies will be needed to ascertain, in each case: (a) To what extent can crops presently grown be replaced by low-water-demand and/or higher value crops? and (b) How much food, especially grain, should be imported?

Storage of flood runoff, aimed at increasing the AR, is already widely practiced. The development of additional storage by means of dams is not promising since the best sites have already been developed. The only practical alternative is to make better use of the AR through conservation (includes reduction of per capita domestic use), reduction of losses caused by pollution and increase of efficiency of irrigation, which is by far the biggest water user.

Fig.1-4 shows where the 250 million irrigated ha in the world are located. Two-thirds of all irrigated land is in the developing countries of which three-fourths are in Asia where, unfortunately, significant reduction of cropland, including irrigated cropland, is taking place due to urbanization and environmental damage.

There is some scope for expansion of I&D in South and Central America, Mexico and Sub-Saharan Africa, primarily in tropical-humid zones. Owing to their wetness, such zones must first be drained. Irrigation can come later, as a *supplement*. Drainage must however be carried out with caution so as to reconcile the conflicting demands of agriculture, urban development, transport and ecosystems. The complications involved are well illustrated by two widely publicized cases: the **Everglades** in Florida and the **Pantanal** in Brazil and Bolivia.[11]

Increasing the Output of Irrigated Agriculture

At a workshop organized by the World Bank, leading irrigation experts from the developing countries gave answers as follows:[12]

- Water losses: Ethiopia: Water losses in some areas reach 40 percent. Jordan: The water system experiences heavy water losses.

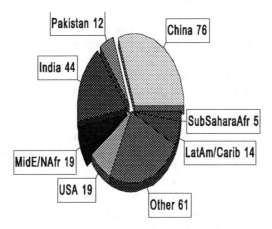

Fig. 1-4. Irrigated Land Areas in the World in millions of hectares (world total is 250 million hectares)

- Sudan: The irrigation system is deteriorating. Mexico: Irrigation efficiencies decreased from 65 percent in 1988 to 40 per cent in 1990. Egypt: Average conveyance losses between the irrigation outlets and the fields are 11 percent, and those between the outlets and the main canal intakes are 25 percent. Although it is not clear from these experts' comments whether water losses could be recovered in downstream areas, from what is known with respect to the configuration of the areas in question, it is not believed that such recovery would be significant, except in the case of Egypt.
- Growing salinity: Iraq: Land lost or impaired by salinity is from 20 to 68 percent. China: In the Yellow River Valley more that three-quarters of the irrigated land has become saline.
- Non-payment of water charges: Egypt: No water charges are collected from farmers, as this is against Islamic precepts. However, in connection with recent physical as well as institutional improvements now underway (pipelines, downstream control on canals and formation of water user associations), some charges are now being introduced to help pay for the improvements. Turkey: As agricultural water is heavily subsidized,

charges are now being introduced to help pay for the improvements. Turkey: As agricultural water is heavily subsidized, water-use efficiency suffers. Thailand: There are laws concerning water charges but they're not enforced owing to frequent changes in government and lack of political will. Pakistan: Cost recoveries are too meager to cover even the usual O&M expenses; which results in progressive deterioration of supply systems. Another Pakistani expert, S.S. Kirmani (he was recipient of the prestigious Tipton Award of the ASCE in 1988, had directed the mammoth Indus Basin Project in Pakistan and later became a high-level official of the World Bank) summarized the current food situation in Pakistan as follows: "Though agricultural production in Pakistan increased sdramatically in the Green Revolution years of the sixties, the country was unable to sustain growth and is currently struggling to achieve self-sufficiency in food. Edible imports are skyrocketing. . . Pakistan and Thailand are the only two countries in Asia that could export food on a sustainable basis. . .but studies emphasize that realizing this potential lies in improving current water and farm management practices, and agricultural inputs and services."

- Poor inter-agency coordination: Sudan: Coordination is poor between two key agencies: one that manages the major canals and secondary canals, and the other that manages tertiary and smaller canals. Senegal: Efforts to reclaim the Senegal River valley have not succeeded owing to lack of central authority at the regional level and excessive, uncoordinated intervention at the national level.
- Neglect of high-value crops: Egypt: About 30 percent of the irrigation supply goes to rice and sugarcane. Although profitable to the farmer who gets free water, these crops are too expensive from a social perspective. Sudan: The country's self-sufficiency policy leads to mismanagement of water and its use for low-value crops.
- Neglect of pilot projects: Egypt: Urgent steps are needed to establish pilot projects on the use of treated wastewater.

A former President of the International Commission for Irrigation and Drainage (ICID), John Hennessy, in a keynote address in 1992 said: "Irrigation schemes in many parts of the world are known to be performing well below their full potential. . . [There is now] wide recognition that deficiencies in management and related institutional *technology* needs greater emphasis. Whatever the final outcome of this debate, it is important that both viewpoints receive full consideration; see the final chapter.[7]

Notes

1. William Bender and Margaret Smith, "Population, Food, and Nutrition," *Population Bulletin, Vol. 51, No.4,* February 1997, Population Reference Bureau, Inc., Washington, D.C., 7-8.

2. "Feeding the World," *IIMI Review, 1994.* International Irrigation Management Institute, Colombo, Sri Lanka, Table 1.

3. World Bank, Washington, D.C., *World Development Report, 1997,* Table 1.

4. Selected leading authorities that have made forecasts of global and regional demand and supply of food:
- Lester Brown (editor) *State of the World, 1998,* W.W. Norton & Co., New York, Chapt. 1.
- Population Information Program, Johns Hopkins Univ., Baltimore, Report Series M, Number 13, *Winning the Food Race,* Dec. 1997.
- Malin Falkenmark and Carl Widstrand "Population and Water Resources: A Delicate Balance," *Population Bulletin, Vol. 47, No. 3,* November 1992, Population Reference Bureau, Washington, D.C.
- Hans W. Wolter and Arumugan Kandiah (Chief and Senior Officer, respectively; Water Resources, Development and Management Services, Land and Water Division, FAO) "Harnessing Water to Feed a Hungry World," *ICID Journal,* 1997, Vol 46, No. 1, 1-20.
- "Reseeding the Green Revolution," *Science,* 22 Aug 1997, Vol. 277, 1038, 1043.·
- "Food Shortages a Real Threat, World Bank Warns; Changes in Agricultural Production Policies Urged," *World Bank News,* April 25, 1996, 5.
- Shlomo Reutlinger and Anne Marie del Castillo "Addressing Hunger: A Historical Perspective of International Initiatives" Appendix 2 in "Overcoming Global Hunger" *Environmentally Sustainable Development Series No. 3,* World Bank, 1994.
- "Overcoming Global Hunger" Proceedings of a Conference on Actions to Reduce Hunger Worldwide," Ismail Serageldin and Pierre Landell-Mills (World Bank), editors, 1994, 243 pages.

Reduce Hunger Worldwide," Ismail Serageldin and Pierre Landell-Mills (World Bank), editors, 1994, 243 pages.

---

5. "Feeding the World" and "Will the World Starve?" *The Economist,* Nov. 16, 1996, 18, 21-23.

6. Lester Brown (editor) *State of the World, 1995,* W.W. Norton & Co., New York

7. Jikun Huang et al "China's Food Economy to the Twenty-First Century: Supply, Demand and Trade," Intl. Food Policy Research Instit., 1997

8. Lester Brown (editor) *State of the World, 1997.* W.W. Norton & Co., New York

9. "Cooking in America—Potential Impacts of Climate Change," Darren Goetze and Elizabeth Farnsworth, *Nuceus,* vol. 20, No. 3, 1-3, Fall 1998, and "A Small price to Pay" Warren Leon, 4-5.

10. "Human Appropriation of Renewable Fresh Water," Sandra Postel, Gretchen C. Daily and Paul R. Ehrlich, *Science,* 9 February 1996, vol. 271, 785-788.

11. J.S. Wade et al "Comparative Analysis of the Florida Everglades and the South American Pantanal" *Proc. Interamerican Dialogue for Water Management,* South Florida Water Management District, Oct.27-30, 1993, 31-70.

12. World Bank. Technical Paper No. 175, *Country Experiences with Water Resources Management—Economic, Institutional and Environmental Issues, 1992.*

Chapter 2

WHAT IS MEANT BY "WATER MANAGEMENT?"

The term "water management" is sometimes limited to mean control of water flows within a specific water-distribution system such as a pipe network or a canal network. For the developed countries, a definition of such limited scope may suffice in some cases, for example, that of a viable, well-established, generally small-scale system with few if any problems of an economic, social or environmental nature. However, nowadays, even in the developed countries, these kinds of problems are coming to the fore, necessitating a *holistic approach*, as many writers have advocated.[1]

The Holistic Nature of Water Management

The use of a holistic approach for dealing with the aforementioned kinds of problems is essential in the case of the developing countries, much more so than for the developed countries.[2][3] This is due to several factors that prevail in the irrigated-agriculture sector of the former but not of the latter, among which are:
- minuscule size of landholdings
- large numbers of landless farmers
- low level of education (particularly of women)
- lack of organized sectors for provision of inputs and for marketing of outputs

- environmental hazards like soil erosion and salinization, loss of forests, and damage to fisheries.

For the developed countries, therefore, a rather broad definition of the term "water management"—as applied to irrigated agriculture—is essential. In this book, the term "water management" is taken as embracing *all* facets of management including:
- Operation and maintenance (O&M) of the development's existing physical infrastructure.
- Arrangements for sharing water with other sectors such as domestic water supply, industrial water supply and hydroelectric power
- Arrangements for sharing revenues and costs with these sectors
- Planning for future modification and/or expansion of the development taking environmental as well as economic factors into account. Among the environmental factors to be considered are preservation of water quality, and conservation of soils, forests, fish and wildlife. The economic factors should include determination of (a) benefits to farmers for various sizes of holding and (b) benefit to the overall economy; concurrently, discussions should be held with officials at the national level to evaluate—and perhaps modify—the effect of macro-economic factors such as taxes and subsidies for imports and exports.
- Arrangements for provision of inputs needed for successful operations. In the case of irrigation projects, for example, these inputs would include seeds, fertilizers and pesticides.
- Arrangements, if needed, for marketing of products produced by the users.
- Arrangements, if needed, for short-term and long-term credit for users.
- Planning and implementation of pilot projects aimed to test and demonstrate to users alternative means of carrying out the foregoing.
- Arrangements for cooperation with overlapping agencies at both local and national levels.
- Arrangements for formation of users' groups, including the means of providing technical assistance to the groups and collection of user charges.
- Administration and personnel management designed to provide incentives for good performance of staff and to prevent corruption.
- Financial controls including amortization of debt, and instruments for financing of future modifications and/or expansions.
- Public relations efforts aimed to convince the general public of the

soundness of the development from various points of view including economic benefits and protection of the environment.

• Arrangements for local participation in all of the foregoing.

The implementation period (time from start of construction to realization of benefits) of a large irrigation project—one larger than say 10,000 ha—may have to be stretched out over a long period of time—say more than five years, which introduces a further complication that has to be dealt with. Quite often it will be necessary to construct and implement a large project in stages, or a particular, large development may have to be planned as a *series of projects*. The sequence of operations in either case should be in the form of a *"Framework Plan."*

The term *Master Plan,* used by some practitioners, can, owing to its ring of finality, be misleading and even dangerous. Large water-resource developments must pass through stages of implementation involving considerable trial-and-error in order to adjust to (not fully foreseen) social, environmental and economic and even technical factors. The term *"Framework Plan"* is more flexible and implies that periodic changes in the plan can be made from time to time as needed.

Whatever term is used, the plan must consider concurrently—in holistic fashion—all the factors listed above. That is not to say that all actions have to be carried out concurrently, only that they have to be *considered and planned concurrently.*

To carry out water management effectively, leadership of high quality and of broad vision is required. Finding and/or training such leadership is of course not easy, but is essential for success of any sizeable development. About this the closing chapter will have more to say after having discussed how this matter was handled (or *not* handled) in actual cases.

The critical importance to the developing countries of sound water planning was brilliantly highlighted in an article by the eminent British economist, Barbara Ward.[4] Her article, aptly titled "Ariadne's Liquid Thread," reported on a major UN conference held in 1977 in Mar del Plata, Argentina. A paragraph in her article justified the title she adopted.

So the UN water conference has to devise proposals for action which recognize that a greatly increased emphasis on water can be one of the main strands in a new, more equitable and hence less politically and socially disruptive pattern of development. Whichever aspect of inadequacy one picks out—the lack of emphasis on safe water, sanitation and health, the enormous neglect of agriculture, the unplanned, pellmell urbanisation and the careless wastes and pollutions of new technologies—water can be

Ariadne's thread through the labyrinth.

Intranational Conflicts Over Scarce Water

Conflicts over scarce water within particular countries are becoming serious in developed as well as in developing countries. The conflicts are either among various land areas in the same sector, e.g., irrigation, or among sectors: irrigation, urban, industry and the environment (including fish and wildlife). Irrigation, being the leading water consumer, is the sector usually identified as the one requiring the greatest effort to conserve water by improving the *efficiency* of irrigation. The term "efficiency" as applied to irrigation can be tricky as there are situations where, even though water losses occur owing to wasteful practices, the loss may not be serious if downstream areas can recover the losses.[5] (See more on this in the final chapter.)

Among the serious ongoing conflicts in the developing world are those of India, described in Chapter 3, and China. In China's case, the conflicts are among sectors and are occurring as a result of rapid urbanization and increased water demand by industry.[6][7]

Noteworthy cases in the U.S.A., as in California and Florida, have been well documented but are of limited value as guidance for the developing countries, for reasons cited earlier in this chapter.

International Conflicts Over Scarce Water

Two leading ongoing and potentially crucial water conflicts are those of the Ganges/Padma River in India/Bangladesh and of the Middle East. These are serious conflicts with more of a *political* rather than a *technical* nature. As will be discussed in Chapters 3 and 9, while technical studies and conferences should by all means be continued, it has to be recognized from the start that little progress in arriving at solutions can be expected without the active participation of important world political leaders.

Notes

1. Some of the authorities that have advocated holistic approaches:
- Neil S. Grigg, "Management Framework for Large-Scale Water Problems," *J. Water Resource Planning & Management, ASCE* 122(4), 1996, 296-300.
- William Whipple, Jr., "Integration of Water Resources Planning and Environmental Regulation," *J. Water Resources Planning & Management,* ASCE, 122(3),

1996."Water Resources: A New Era for Coordination," *ASCE Press*, 1998.
- Neil S. Grigg, discussion of the foregoing, *J. Water Resources Planning & Management*, ASCE, 123, 1997, 197-198.
- Warren Viessman, Jr. and Claire Welty, "Water Management: Technology and Institutions," Harper & Row, New York, 1985.
- Neil S. Grigg, "Water Resources Management: Principles, Regulations, and Cases", McGraw-Hill Book Co., New York, 1996.

2. Phillip Z. Kirpich, "Holistic Approach to Irrigation Management in Developing Countries," *J. Irrig. & Drainage Engrng.*, ASCE, 119(2), 1993, 323-333.

3. Water Resources Research (1993). *Special Section: Water Resources Issues and Problems in Developing Countries* American Geophysical Union, Washington, DC 20009, July 1993. Paper #1, D.S. Brookshire and D. Whittington, "Water Resources Issues in the Developing Countries." Paper #2, C.W. Howe and J.A. Dixon,"Inefficiencies in Water Project Design and Operation in the Third World: An Economic Perspective." Paper #3, P. Roger et al,"Water Resources Planning in a Strategic Context: Linking the Water Sector to the National Economy." Paper #4 Eleanor Ostrom, "Design Principles in Long-Enduring Irrigation Institutions." Paper #5, K. William Easter,"Economic Failure Plagues Developing Countries' Public Irrigation: An Assurance Problem."

4. Barbara Ward, "Ariadne's Thread", *The Economist*, February 5, 1977.

5. David Seckler, Director General, International Irrigation Management Institute (IIMI), Research Report 1, *The New Era of Water Resource Management: From "Dry" to "Wet" Water Savings*, 1996, IIMI, Colombo, Sri Lanka.

6. Zhang Zezhen et al, "Challenges to and Opportunities for Development of China'sWater Resources in the 21st Century," *Water International, 17 (1992)*, 21-27.

7. Lester R. Brown,"Who Will Feed China?" 1995, Chapters I-5, W.W. Norton & Co., New York.

Chapter 3

LESSONS FROM PAST CASES, SOUTH AND EAST ASIA

China, India and Pakistan, the three largest countries in the region, have an aggregate irrigated area of 132 million ha. Adding 3 million ha for Bangladesh, gives a total for these four countries of 136 million ha. Figures are not readily available for the other countries in the region that have sizeable irrigated areas including Sri Lanka, Thailand, Myanmar, Vietnam, Taiwan, the Philippines and Indonesia. Adding them would bring the total for South and East Asia to well over half that for the world as a whole.

As China was visited by the author only as a tourist, it is not discussed further in this chapter. China is the leading country in the world in terms of area irrigated and is a special case in view of its high economic growth rate and breakneck speeds of industrialization and urbanization. From the point of view of the global supply of food, China may pose a serious problem for the world, as was intimated in Chapters 1 and 2; see also the final chapter.

Bangladesh

Population in 1997: 122,000,000
Population in 2025: 180,000,000
Fertility rate: 3.6
Per capita GNP (US$): 240

Population growth rate: 2.0%
Area: 143,000 km^2
Life expectancy: 58 years
Percent urban: 16

Bangladesh, with an area about that of Florida (but with ten times the population), is an extensive, flat floodplain less than 9 m above sea level,

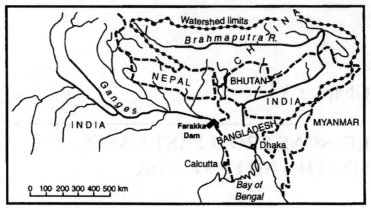

Fig. 3-1. The Brahmaputra-Ganges Delta in Bangladesh

located in a highly fertile delta formed by sediments from two major rivers: the Ganges and the Brahmaputra (Fig. 3-1). The Ganges (called the Padma in Bangladesh) originates in India while the Brahmaputra originates in China and India.

Water to Bangladesh is both a blessing and a curse. Heavy monsoon rainfall causes the rivers to overflow every year. Then follow 4 to 5 months of relative dryness. Of the annual rainfall of 1,500 to 2,500 mm, from 1,300 to 2,000 mm fall during the monsoon, normally from June to October. Dry spells occur fairly frequently during the monsoon causing need for irrigation of the rice crop even during the monsoon.

The Bangladeshis have adapted to the annual monsoon flooding (Fig. 3-2) by placing their villages on mounds. Their houses are thus protected against the average—but not extreme—monsoon floods. They plant a variety of rice (called "floating rice" or "*broadcast aman*") that grows a bit faster than the rise in the flood waters, often reaching a height of six feet; but it is low-yielding in terms of kg per ha. Farmers are acquainted with other varieties that give greater yields but are reluctant to change owing to the risk of dry spells during the monsoon. Where irrigation has been introduced, farmers have attained per-crop yields of 2 to 2.5 tons per ha. Although not high by world standards, such yields are much higher

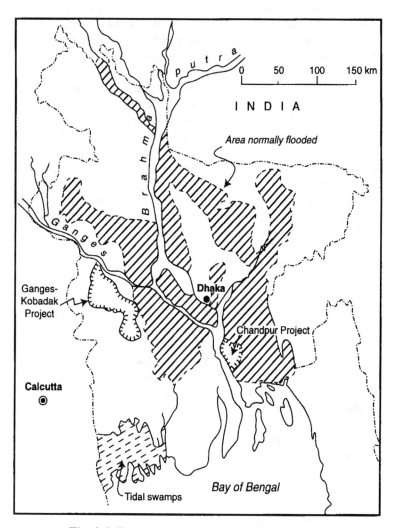

Fig. 3-2. Bangladesh: Area Normally Flooded

than for broadcast aman. Given the high fertility of the soils, it is possible with complete water control to grow at least two and up to three crops a year. The three types of high-yielding varieties in use are: *Transplanted aman,* during the monsoon; *Aus,* pre-monsoon, March to July; and *Boro,* during the dry winter months, from November to March.

In addition to flooding from overflow of the rivers, serious floods occur periodically in coastal zones caused by cyclones (hurricanes) in the Bay of Bengal. One such flood occurred in November 1970 when the author, who was in the country on a World Bank mission, was flown over the flooded areas in a helicopter and could see the bodies of dead people (the death toll was about half a million!) and of cattle, strewn the length of the coastal zone. The only practicable defenses against such floods are properly designed shelters with floor levels a few feet higher than the maximum tidal surge experienced in the past. A series of such shelters, of concrete, were constructed during the 1980s.

Large-Scale vs. Small-Scale Projects

Much foreign technical assistance has flowed into Bangladesh during the past five decades, following the end in 1947 of the British presence. Prior to 1971, when East Pakistan broke away from Pakistan and became the independent nation of Bangladesh, some of this assistance came from arid West Pakistan as well, where physical and socio-economic conditions were quite different. Misguided assistance from foreign sources including West Pakistan resulted in some projects that were *not* suited to the conditions in Bangladesh.

An example is the **Ganges-Kobadak (GK) Project** serving 140,000 ha (Fig. 3-2). The project includes a major pumping station, on the Ganges River, which discharges into a gravity system including a main supply canal. The system is operated to supply *supplemental water* for cultivation of the *transplanted aman* and *aus* crops. There is no attempt to supply water during the dry winter months for a *boro* crop, as practiced elsewhere in Bangladesh.

The pumping station, despite its sophisticated design, continues to suffer from serious siltation of its intake. The main canal had initially been subject to serious leakage through its containing embankments which, had not been adequately compacted; and right-of-way acquisition had caused abandonment of many small holdings. Performance of the project for supply of water for the *aman* and *aus* crops has improved in recent years.[1]

Since it is generally plentiful in most of Bangladesh, use of groundwater would have been an obvious alternative to a gravity system. A groundwater-based system would moreover have been able to supply water for a *boro* crop. However, even if such a system had been proposed, the East Pakistan Water and Power Authority (EPWAPDA— the predecessor of the Bangladesh Water Development Board) would have been strongly opposed. EPWAPDA wanted major gravity-canal systems that require large, *monumental* structures, not puny shallow wells, and EPWAPDA, strongly supported by the national government in Islamabad and by the provincial government in Dhaka, wanted to establish a claim for rights to a fair share of the waters of the Ganges.

Since the existing gravity system of the GK Project is not operated at all during the boro season and only partially during the aus season, utilizing groundwater as a supplement to the surface water might be highly advantageous. Use of both sources—surface water and groundwater—has been successful in the Indian states of Punjab, Haryana and Gujarat, where climatic conditions are similar but, on the other hand, where farmers have been assisted through cheap electricity for pumping and through low-interest credit.

India, by about 1980, completed construction of the Farakka Barrage on the Ganges for the purpose of diverting some of the river's flow to the Hooghly River, which is actually an estuary leading to the harbor of Calcutta. India claims it needs this water in order to flush sediments that are clogging the harbor. Protracted negotiations between the two countries concerning water rights have led nowhere. Recently however there are some hopeful signs that a settlement may be reached (*The Economist*, November 6, 1996, 37). A dream scheme of B.A. Abbas, a leading past chairman of EPWAPDA, was to build a major feeder canal that would draw water from the upper reaches of the Brahmaputra River in India and convey the water to the Ganges River just downstream of the Farakka Barrage. This would be a truly monumental undertaking. As far as is known, not even preliminary studies of this idea have been started.

By 1975, EPWAPDA, followed by BWDB, was able to equip only 32,000 ha with canal-served systems. A rival government agency, the

Agricultural Development Corporation (ADC) took a different approach, which was to install small, low-lift pumps on perennial streams and to drill and equip small wells utilizing shallow groundwater. By 1975 they had installed 35,000 such low-lift pumps reaching 700,000 ha or twenty times what BWDB had reached. A recent published report shows that this large gravity schemes on the other has continued.[2]

Irrigation Method	1978	1991
Low-lift pumps	500,000 ha	600,000 ha
Shallow wells	100,000 ha	1,100,000 ha
Deep tubewells	200,000 ha	600,000 ha
Traditional	700,000 ha	600,000 ha
Large-scale canal	100,000 ha	100,000 ha
TOTAL	1,600,000 ha	3,000,000 ha

The low-lift pumps and the small diesel engines that drive them are mounted on the same frame, making a pumpset. Their capacity is about 50 liters per second (2 cubic feet per second), which can serve up to 50 ha of land. This relatively low area per unit of water flow is due in part to the extreme fragmentation of land that prevails. In many parts of Bangladesh the average landholding is only 0.8 ha and this is often fragmented into as many as ten pieces so that the plot size is often only 0.08 ha (800 m^2 for a plot of about 40 x 20 m). Population growth and customs regarding inheritance are part of the explanation for the fragmentation but another perhaps more important reason is the fact that farmers like to have land at different elevations as a form of insurance against the vagaries of flood and drought. A low-lying plot is subject to flooding but is less likely to suffer from drought in the dry season, while a plot on relatively high ground is free from flooding but more subject to drought damage.

The small landholding size and its fragmentation greatly complicate water distribution and collection of water charges. ADC established "pump groups" to handle these matters, with each pump group supplying water to from 60 to 100 farmers. A so-called *Thana Irrigation Plan* (TIP) was set up for each *thana* (the basic unit of government, of which there are about 500 in the country) whereby the responsibility for forming pump groups was assigned to local-government civil authorities.

The pumpsets have been located along perennial streams with suitable streambanks for siting of the pumpsets. Additional sites were selected along natural drainage channels that discharge to the perennial streams; such sites have sometimes required minor excavation which was carried out under rural works programs, some of which have been financed by foreign NGOs. Purchase of diesel fuel and maintenance of the pumps and engines has been carried out by the pump groups with spare parts and technical assistance provided by ADC.

The way in which the TIP low-lift pump program has been organized is significant as it indicates that even subsistence farmers are willing to share in the cost of irrigation. Moreover, these farmers gain, at an early stage, a sense of participation in the irrigation scheme since they assist in the planning of the distribution system in their area and also contribute their labor and some land.

Where perennial surface water is available, the use of low-lift pumps is clearly the most economical form of irrigation in Bangladesh. In the 1970s it was estimated that the per hectare costs of low-lift pumping, deep tubewells and large-scale gravity-canal projects would be respectively $80, $700 and $1,000.

"Master Plans"

Through loans and credits, the World Bank supported ADC's small-scale irrigation but was under strong political pressure to support BWDB as well in its efforts to launch large-scale projects. These included major embanking of the Ganges and Brahmaputra Rivers and more big gravity-canal schemes, like Ganges-Kobadak. In the 1960s the Bank had in fact financed two projects involving major embankments, one for protection of the capital city, Dhaka, and the second, known as the "Brahmaputra Right Bank Project" for protection of an agricultural area of 200,000 ha in a zone about 200 km long on the right bank of that river.

Beginning in the mid-1960s up to the mid-1980s, the Bank financed, sometimes in cooperation with UNDP, major studies aimed at determining how best to proceed in the medium and long term. The author was heavily involved from 1963 to 1972, during which period the Bank set up a team of five, headed by an administrator, plus four staff members representing the pertinent disciplines: macro-economics, micro-economics, agriculture and engineering (the author).

The initial assignment of the team was to review a massive, so-called "Master Plan" prepared by International Engineering Co. (IECO) of San Francisco. IECO's study, which had been promoted and paid for by

USAID. (For reasons given in Chapter 2, the term "Master Plan" is inappropriate and even misleading; the term "Framework Plan" is preferable.) IECO's master plan, which was based largely on California experience, assumed that all that was necessary was a series of diversion dams and large gravity canals. But serious questions were left unanswered. How would floods be controlled? Could the rivers be pinched by embankments without ill effects? How would land needed for the embankments be obtained, with the multiplicity of small landowners that would have to vacate? For dry-season irrigation, how would costs compare with water pumped from shallow wells? The team's judgement was that the IECO master plan was of little or no use.

With the team's assistance, another firm was engaged: Acres International, of Canada, to act as "General Consultants," mainly to supervise the work of "Project Consultants" who were doing the planning for the larger-scale projects. The team also made use of their services in preparing the terms of reference for "Regional Studies" of each of the four regions into which the country was subdivided. Each Regional Study would be carried out by a world-rank firm/agency in the field of water-resource planning, including SOGREAH of France, the Rijkswaterstaat of the Netherlands and the U.S. Bureau of Reclamation. A prestigious "Ad Hoc Flood Consulting Panel" was selected and gave its assistance to the team in preparing the terms of reference.

Negotiations were carried out to the point of initialing of the relevant contracts but then all of this *advance planning for planning* came to naught when it had to be aborted owing to the hostilities between East and West Pakistan beginning about mid-1971. India intervened and East Pakistan became independent, changing its name to Bangladesh. One of the reasons for East Pakistan's discontent could have been in part the previously mentioned disastrous floods of November 1970.

In the years 1983-1986, more master planning was carried out when the Harza Engineering Co. of Chicago, with funding from the UNDP, was engaged to prepare a "Water Sector Master Plan." A three-man evaluation team engaged by the UNDP in late-1986, of which the author was a part, reviewed the results of Harza's work and found it inconsequential, although the Harza report did stress the importance and priority of what was already happening, namely, concentration on small-scale development based on low-lift pumps and shallow wells. On the other hand, the Harza report gave lip service to the large-scale projects, with the qualification that they would need more study.

In 1987 and 1988 disastrous floods occurred and in June 1989 the World Bank complied with a request from the Bangladesh Government to provide help in coordinating international efforts, which at that point consisted of studies sponsored by France, Japan and the United States (USAID). The relative World Bank document, which appeared December 11, 1989,[3] stated in its background introduction that all of the then-current studies recommended caution with respect to further embanking of the major rivers and all recommended many more studies.

A more recent report concerning long-range water planning for Bangladesh, referred to earlier in this chapter, was that of December 1994 by Peter Roger and a team of experts. This report, whose cost was paid by USAID, contains a useful summary of the then current situation, which is, in fact rather confusing in view of the current *independent studies,* either just terminating or still going on:

- *Eastern Water Study* by USAID through the Irrigation Support Group for Asia and the Near East, prepared basically by the same team headed by Peter Rogers and completed in 1989
- The World Bank document of December 1989 previously referred to: "Bangladesh: Action Plan for Flood Control"
- A study by Bangladeshi experts in cooperation with UNDP
- A study by a French Engineering Consortium with Bangladeshi collaboration
- A study by the Japanese International Cooperation Agency
- The report by Peter Roger et al of December 1994

The Peter Roger et al report presents recommendations on priorities for the short and medium term, giving emphasis to groundwater development for at least the next ten years, while counseling caution with respect to major embanking of the main rivers. (The disastrous 1993 flood of the Mississippi River had further alerted river-control experts to the reality that flood embankments, while still needed to protect high-density urban areas, may otherwise be a detriment.) The report makes a plea for better cooperation between BWDB, which is still oriented in favor of large-scale projects and other agencies, although the report fails to mention ADC, the key agency that handled the largely successful low-lift-pump and shallow-well programs. The report also asks that BWDB pay more attention to growing problems of urban and industrial water supply, which certainly has much importance since much of the future of Bangladesh will entail shifting its overwhelmingly high rural population (now 84 percent) into industrially based cities.

A situation apparently not considered in the Peter Rogers et al report is that of the Brahmaputra River in the Assam Valley of India, which is upstream of Bangladesh. This major valley, which is about 600 km long, is subject to periodic serious floods. The Indians are studying ways to control these floods,[4] including major embankments that, if built, could result in large increases in flooding downstream in Bangladesh.

L. Douglas James, who worked for ISPAN, wrote an article in which he emphasized the importance, in any case, of increased utilization of local human resources.[5] (For his article, James received in 1996 the Best Paper Award of IWRA.) In a Letter to the Editor in the same journal, the author heartily concurred with James on this point, while stating that to achieve such utilization also needs a program involving training and incentives for local leaders and better cooperation among the rival national agencies; these include not only BWDB and ADC but also the local civil authorities that report to a different central-government ministry. (The letter also pointed out the urgent need in the case of Bangladesh of internationally-supported family planning programs, but this was left out by the editor of the journal.)

The large volume of foreign technical assistance to Bangladesh, while profitable to foreign experts and consulting firms, has been of limited benefit to Bangladesh. Such assistance must nevertheless be continued since Bangladesh is not able to face its problems unaided. To improve the effectiveness of such assistance will require *coordinated* international backing (including financing), *with only one agency taking the lead as well as the responsibility.* See further comments at the end of this section.

Finding a Synthesis: The Chandpur Project and the Use of Double Lifting

In the late 1960s and early 1970s, it was foreseen that irrigation by means of low-lift pumping would soon reach a ceiling owing to the limited number of perennial streams in the country with sufficient dry-season water flow. Some larger rivers remained with adequate water flows but located too far from the areas to be irrigated to be served by low-lift pumps.

Concurrently, a U.S. (California) consulting engineering firm was engaged in planning a project for possible World Bank financing in the Chandpur Project area, 50,000 ha in extent in the southeast part of the country. The firm was following the conventional gravity-canal-system design as was used at Ganges-Kobadak but was encountering severe difficulty in planning the canal system owing to the multiplicity of small landholdings. The World Bank team, of which the author was a part, were in contact with the firm and together came up with a new idea, namely, to use the natural drainage channels to distribute the irrigation water, thus eliminating the need to take land for canals from the farmers; see Fig. 3-3. This is a highly important consideration in view of the high population density, which is typical in Bangladesh and other Asian countries.

A relatively large (1,200 cusec) fixed primary pumping station was planned and designed, which lifts water from a large perennial nearby stream and discharges the water into the natural drainage channels from which movable low-lift pumps provide a second lift of the water to the farmers' plots. Chandpur is actually a *polder*, as it includes a peripheral flood-protection embankment 95 km long and 4 to 5 m high. The revised design included: ponds for raising fingerlings, as worked out with the Fisheries Department in order to preserve the livelihood of 3,000 fishermen in the area; and navigation locks to permit access to small boats that navigate the natural drainage channels.

Since completion, in about 1978, land-use intensity (number of crops per year) has reached as high as 2.4.[7] Following the favorable outcome of Chandpur, several other projects embodying this idea of *double lifting* were planned and implemented.

Small Polders

Following independence, Bangladesh received some technical assistance from the International Fund for Agricultural Development (IFAD), based in Rome. In 1982 the author was engaged to head a four-man team that, with assistance from a Bangladeshi consulting firm, identified and prepared a feasibility study for a **small polder project** consisting of a series of small polders ranging in size from about 2,000 to 8,000 ha. Operation and maintenance (O&M) would be largely by the local farmers *themselves* with some technical assistance from the Bangladesh Water Board.[8]

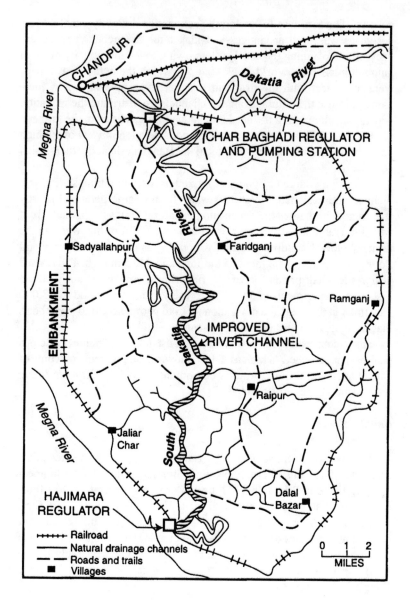

Fig. 3-3. Chandpur Project

Subsequent to issuance by IFAD of the feasibility study, the World Bank agreed to finance the project, but on condition that it be carried out *entirely* by the BWDB. The Bank insisted on this condition despite the IFAD team's observation that O&M by BWDB had largely failed and that a way should be found to get much more direct involvement by local people.

There is wide scope for proceeding with many more small polders, although it is clear that if too many are developed flooding conditions could under various situations be aggravated. Hugh Brammer, an FAO soils expert with long residence in Bangladesh, wrote about the potential for small polders and the author expressed some cautions in a published letter of discussion.[9]

Bangladesh with its high and dense population (which is still growing at the rate of 2.2 percent per annum—doubles every 30 years) and strategic location has world importance. It is imperative for the world to help the country find a way to deal with its social, economic and physical problems. Paramount among these problems are how to manage its water resources. The haphazard and sporadic attempts to date by various foreign donors has provided many lessons that must now be reviewed and taken seriously. A *single* international agency should be chosen and should take full responsibility for providing this help. It should be staffed and funded bearing in mind that, even for experts, complex water planning requires that they *live with the problems* for a sufficiently long period of time! See more about this in the final chapter.

India

Population in 1997: 970,000,000	Population growth rate: 1.9%
Population in 2025: 1,385,000,000	Area: 3,290,000 km^2
Fertility rate: 1.9	Life expectancy: 59 years
Per capita GNP (US$): 340	Percent urban: 26

India in 1987 had 60 million hectares *equipped* for irrigation of which 45 million were actually irrigated. India is second in the world—after China—in terms of area irrigated.

In the 1960s and 1970s, through use of High Yielding Varieties (HYVs) for wheat and rice, India had a food surplus for a few years. This was called "The Green Revolution." The HYVs were the result of improved seeds developed by research stations in Mexico, for wheat and maize (corn), and the Philippines, for rice; these stations are part of the network of agricultural research stations supported by the Consultative Group for International Agricultural Research (CGIAR). (CGIAR receives financial support from the World Bank and from other donors.) But the Green Revolution was not due only to the new HYVs. What is often overlooked is that the HYVs are very sensitive to control of water and must have the right amount—not too much and not too little—at the right time. These optimum water conditions were present in India in the Punjab—India's breadbasket—through a massive program supported by the Bank for the drilling and equipping of shallow wells, as supplemented by an electricity-distribution network to supply energy to the well pumps. In fact, since the late 1970s India's grain production has not increased because water availability has become a constraint, although there are other reasons.

Groundwater in the Punjab being such a valuable resource, but one that was in danger of being over-exploited, the author managed to interest the National Government and the State Governments in a major agricultural study which would concentrate on determining how the supply of groundwater could be increased, possibly from deepwells rather than from the existing shallow wells. The study would have been carried out by an Indian team with support for the groundwater investigations from the U.S. Bureau of Reclamation (USBR). Financing of the study would have been included in a loan being negotiated for a Second Stage Drainage Project for Punjab and Haryana. Negotiations with USBR were carried out and agreement on a contract almost reached when the process got interrupted and then shelved indefinitely because of the tense situation arising with Pakistan.

System Deficiencies

As a member of a three-man Study Team set up by CGIAR in 1981 and 1982, and which led to the formation of the International Irrigation Management Institute (IIMI), the author had the unique opportunity to observe and meet with leading Indian officials and to learn from them what they considered these deficiencies to be.[10]

As these officials themselves pointed out, their massive irrigation system suffers from many deficiencies, which, broadly speaking, are of two classes: *physical* and *managerial.* The physical ones include such items as faulty or absent control structures, inadequate canal capacity in relation to peak demand, inadequate rural road networks, lack of telecommunications and poor operation and maintenance (O&M). The managerial ones—usually more difficult to solve—include:

- Lack of adequate farmers' organizations at the local level—made difficult by the prevalence of very small landholdings.
- Low incentives for staff of the State Irrigation Departments to operate the systems effectively. Salaries are low and the operating staffs are notorious for their bribe-taking!
- Jealousy resulting in disputes among the State Irrigation Departments, the State Agriculture Departments and the Command Area Development Authorities (CADAs). The CADAs were set up in the 1970s as independent State agencies with administrators chosen from the elite Indian Administrative Service, without background in either irrigation or agriculture.

In the 1970s, 44 CADAs were set up covering 74 major canal commands serving 15 million ha. But the CADAs had only limited success. The reasons, generally well-understood by Indian officials, concern faulty enterprise/management-type practices, faults in the main-canal system (insufficient or untimely water deliveries), lack of roads and drainage, and lack of advice to farmers on appropriate farming systems.

As cited by leading Indian officials and as the author was able to corroborate through interviews with local and foreign experts based in India (WB, UNDP, USAID and Ford Foundation), current deficiencies include:

Main system:
- Control structures too few or of inadequate design. Canals are run either completely full or completely off.
- Canal capacity inadequate in relation to peak demand and less than original owing to poor maintenance.
- System operation based on water availability rather than water demand.
- Lack of telecommunications
- Lack of interest (and incentive) of State Irrigation Departments' staffs in O&M. Setting up of separate O&M wings in these departments is under consideration.

On-farm systems

- Lack of coordination in each State among the Irrigation Department, the CADAs and the Agriculture Department. Failure to appoint a head to direct rather than merely coordinate
- The CADAs have inadequate administrative powers.
- The CADA administrators, often chosen from the elite Indian Administrative Service, are too junior, lack leadership qualities or lack background in irrigation and agriculture and are therefore resented by old hands in the <u>Irrigation and Agriculture Departments</u>.
- Inadequate training in on-farm water management due to lack of curricula in the universities and lack of in-service training.
- Known technologies of water distribution are not applied. The usual current methods are plot-to-plot and flood irrigation. Borders and furrows are rarely used.
- Project outlets serve blocks of 40 ha, which often serve as many as 20 to 40 farmers. The Central Government has requested the States to extend project canals to serve 5 to 8 ha but this program is controversial and moves very slowly.
- Research is lacking (and farmers therefore not receiving advice) on appropriate farming systems either under existing conditions of deficient water supply or improved conditions.

The following extracts from a recent article in *The Economist* and another from *The Journal of Development Studies* of 1982 are worth quoting:

> Irrigation. . .During the British raj, canal charges provided a commercial rate of return on investment. Today revenues cover only 7.5% of the cost of operating and maintaining irrigation systems. The subsidy costs the taxpayer 23 billion rupees ($735 m) a year, and there is not enough money for repairing or desilting canals, so the whole canal network is deteriorating.
> Canal charges are levied not on the volume of water a farmer uses but on the area he irrigates. So farmers in the upper reaches of canals have an incentive to grow thirsty crops such as rice and sugar cane, depriving farmers farther along the canal of water, years of excessive soaking of the land have led to waterlogging and salinity, turning irrigation into a curse instead of a benefit.[11]

The paper describes how some irrigation engineers raise vast amounts of illicit revenue from the distribution of water and contracts, and redistribute part to superior officers and politicians. It argues that the corruption 'system' which is centered on control of personnel transfers, is an important supply-side reason for poor performance of canal-irrigated agriculture. Insofar as the same system operates in other government departments, it may be more important for understanding Indian politics and the political influence on economic development than has previously been realised.[12]

The foregoing list and quotes show that while there are many technical deficiencies, the more serious and difficult ones to correct are people-related. Innovative management will be needed to find ways to overcome bureaucratic inertia and vested interests and to change malpractices of long duration such as running canals completely full or completely off and on-farm water distribution by plot-to-plot or by flooding. The technical deficiencies can be corrected through use of technologies already known although there are opportunities for high-tech applications in telecommunications and regulators in the larger canals.

Narmada Development

This development (Fig. 3-4), currently underway, is both very large and controversial. Its aim is utilization of the waters of the Narmada River to provide irrigation for over 2 million ha while generating a large amount of badly needed electrical energy. During the years 1978 to 1983, following his retirement from the World Bank, the author assisted as a consultant on development planning as part of a team that included specialists in agriculture, economics and groundwater.

The team met frequently with staff of the Irrigation Departments of Gujarat and Madhya Pradesh, the two States mainly involved. These two States plus two adjoining ones had quarreled over allocation of the river's waters and a special high-level court had adjudicated the issue, which had taken ten years to accomplish. Although progress was achieved in reaching agreement on planning procedures, several issues remained unresolved, including:

- Phasing. The area to be developed—two million hectares—is too large for development in a single phase. A phased development would cause delay in construction of some of the dams and, more importantly, would call for phased construction of the very large and complex Main Canal.

- There are two areas that should be deferred or perhaps eliminated: One, which is on the west side at a relatively high elevation, would require expensive pumping. The other is largely a marsh near the mouth of the Narmada River. Both have been included for political reasons but at most likely excessive cost.
- Intensity of irrigation: There is not enough water to irrigate the entire area at high intensity. Will the developers plan to spread the waters thinly, just to serve more farmers or, instead, serve fewer farmers adequately?
- *Firm* arrangements are lacking for farmers to pay for (a) capital costs and (b) operation and maintenance costs, the latter to prevent future deterioration?

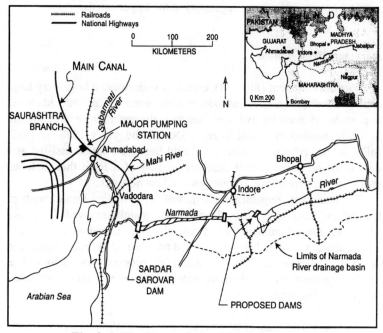

Fig. 3-4. The Narmada Development in India

- Action as well as planning is lacking with respect to the large Tawa area in area in Madhya Pradesh wherein irrigation canals have been provided despite serious drainage problems, whose olution in the author's view should take precedence over irrigation.

The development requires building several major dams. The dams, as is usually the case, require the removal and resettlement of several

---

The demarcation line between India and Pakistan, as agreed in 1947, went through the Punjab, wherein is located the best agricultural land in either country. The Punjab Water System was dismembered by this line, and this caused serious disputes between the two countries.

India was in control of the headwaters. Nehru said at first that what India did with its rivers was strictly India's business but later invited David Lilienthal—see the section on Colombia in Chapter 6—to give advice on how to proceed. An article by Lilienthal, outlining his ideas, appeared in *Colliers,* a magazine; it was read by Eugene Black, a close friend of Lilienthal's and President of the World Bank. Black reacted positively and put the resources of the Bank to work to help in the negotiations to end the dispute. The negotiations, which took ten years, called for major *link canals* to transfer water from the eastern tributaries of the Indus to Pakistan, plus two major dams: *Mangla* and *Tarbela.* Financing of these works was to a major extent by grants from the Western countries.

The Tarbela dam, on the main Indus River, was very costly—in the neighborhood of $2 billion or twice the original estimate. The reservoir formed by the dam has limited life owing to a high rate of siltation. Whether the dam was economically justified remains an unresolved question. An alternative development based on groundwater pumping might have been far less costly and more economic. The Bank's higher officials, led by Lieftinck, the Dutch Executive Director, may have felt that the political impasse between the two countries dictated approval of the two major dams and that economic justification was only a secondary issue..

Despite the Bank's decision, hostilities broke out anyhow over Kashmir and over East Pakistan which became Bangladesh. Pakistan and India are still hostile and are worried about nuclear bombs in their adversary's hands.

hundred thousand people. The world environmental movement got wind of this and lodged strong protests, which, despite earlier close involvement with the scheme, caused the Bank to withdraw. The Indians said never mind, we'll go ahead on our own.

The Bank's decision to withdraw was, in the view of a former Bank colleague[13] who had spent many years on Narmada, a bad mistake. There are many issues other than resettlement, including those listed above, regarding which the Bank could have exerted a positive influence. (The Bank's influence stems basically from the fact that India is a major borrower of the Bank through Loans and IDA Credits. The latter are loans at practically zero interest, with long forgiveness periods; only countries with large populations *below the poverty line* are eligible for such loans.)

The case against Narmada made by environmentalists is reminiscent of what a guide said in Egypt when, during a visit to one of its ancient monuments whose foundations were being threatened by the rise in the Nile caused by the major Aswan dam (a gift from USSR): "Sure, we don't like this threat to our ancient monuments. But we have no choice. We have to feed our people and the dam enables us to do that!"

Laos

Population in 1997: 5,100,000	Population growth rate: 2.8%
Population in 2025: 9,800,000	Area: 238,000 km^2
Fertility rate: 6.1	Life expectancy: 52 years

The Na Xai Thong Agricultural Development Project

This project provides an example of *monumentalism*, a common affliction among promoters and some engineers. For this project, with an area of 20,000 ha located in the valley of the Nam Ngum River about an hour's drive north of Vientiane, the capital, two dams had already been substantially completed. The next step was to build canals to convey the impounded water to farmers' fields. A feasibility study had been completed in December 1980 by FAO with assistance from the Mekong Committee based in Bangkok, Thailand. The International Fund for Agricultural Development (IFAD) was asked to finance the project for this next stage. In 1981, the author was engaged by IFAD to head a 5-person mission to appraise the project for possible financing. The other four members of the mission were an agronomist, formerly with FAO, an

> Laos, formerly part of French Indochina, is one of the least developed countries in Asia with no railroads, few roads and almost no mining or industry. Since the end of the Vietnam War in 1975, Laos has been increasingly dependent on Vietnam for military and economic assistance.

economist from SIDA, a Swedish agency, and two members of the IFAD staff.

For the dams, a Japanese agency had prepared preliminary designs; final designs were done with assistance from the USSR, and construction was funded from two sources: OPEC and SIDA. From examination of the dams and of the reports on which the designs were based, the mission had doubts concerning design of the earthen embankments that formed the main part of the dams and on the capacity of the concrete spillways to prevent overtopping of the embankments. The 1980 FAO report had expressed similar reservations concerning the safety of the dams.

The mission felt that, besides reviewing the design of the spillways and the embankments, the reservoirs behind each dam should be filled very slowly so that, by means of piezometers (observation pipes), the saturation lines could be observed. It could then be determined whether remedial measures, such as placing heavy porous rock at the toes of the embankments, could be needed.

There were at least three further serious questions: First, two feeder canals, one 5.5 km and the other 10 km long, were still lacking to convey water from the outlet works of each of the dams to the irrigable zone. Both canals will have to traverse difficult sandy and rocky terrain and will have to be protected with concrete linings; their cost, as yet undetermined, will likely be high.

Second, the quantity of water available for irrigation was in doubt owing to lack of hydrologic records of sufficient duration.

Third, the characteristics, both physical and social, of the irrigable zone had not been adequately studied. Of the 20,000 ha in the project area, 13,000 were considered cultivable but, in the absence of a *land classification study*, it was not known how much of this would be irrigable, nor the extent to which land leveling and construction of rural roads would be required.

There were about 20 villages in the area, with about 500 persons per village, located in a low-lying 3,000-ha zone devoted to terraced rice paddies, some of which was subject to flooding from the adjacent Nam Ngum River. We visited the villages and found that despite their subsistence-type agriculture, the villagers were doing quite well. To construct canals for water distribution would be costly and disruptive in view of the villagers' very small holdings.

The 1980 FAO report had expressed additional reservations concerning: drainage problems of the area to be irrigated and flooding from the hilly area west of the project; the irrigation distribution system; the implementation capacity of the government to carry out conventional gravity irrigation systems; and inadequate incentives to farmers to grow other than subsistence crops..

Based on visits to the villages, the mission found this last point to be a very valid one. The farmers were growing almost nothing other than rice for auto consumption. They did have some incentive for growing additional rice but only for barter, not for sale for cash, since there was little they could buy for cash, given the state of the economy. The government was aware of the problem of farmers' incentives but needed time to work out satisfactory solutions. The Na Xai Thong project should be a good place, the mission thought, to start to work out solutions because of its nearness to Vientiane and because a rural electrification project then underway would in the following two or three years provide electricity to the zone for the first time.

With its proximity to the alluvium of the Nam Ngum River, the area, the mission thought, should have ample groundwater. It would have been a fairly simple matter to determine whether this was so. If favorable, a far simpler way would be available to obtain the water needed and without disrupting the villagers' generally favorable ongoing agriculture. At a later stage, after the technical difficulties concerning the dams and the feeder canals had been resolved, and after completion of suitable land-classification mapping, additional irrigation could be planned and implemented.

The mission reached the judgement that development of the entire project area of 13,000 ha would require 15 to 20 years, divided into several stages or "Time slices". Stage I would be carried out over a four-year period, in four parts:

Part 1 - Groundwater explorations
Part 2 - Implementation based on groundwater

Part 3 - Framework planning

Part 4 - Preparation of a Stage II Project.

With electricity available in the villages, installation of wells provides two additional important advantages: the availability of *supplemental irrigation* for irrigation during the monsoon (sometimes the monsoon is late and sometimes there are dry periods during the monsoon)and the provision of potable drinking water to the villages. The wells would be relatively small with capacities of about 10 liters per second and no more than 30 m deep. To energize the wells, low-voltage lines could be extended for a distance of 1 to 2 km from step-down transformers in each village. Each village would then become a *development pole*. Following a reconnaissance, tentative well locations would be selected and an exploratory borehole sunk. If sufficiently favorable conditions were found, the borehole would immediately be converted into a permanent production well serving about 10 ha. Thus Part 2 would proceed concurrently with the groundwater explorations. This manner of proceeding has been used successfully in villages in Mexico; see Chapter 6.

A further important advantage of a system based on small wells rather than one based on gravity canals is that the difficulties and costs of land leveling (to prepare the land for irrigation) is greatly simplified and reduced.

In order to circumvent the problem of implementation capacity, the mission proposed to the Laotian authorities that responsibility for Stage I (all four parts) be assigned to an expatriate consulting group from a nearby country that has similar ecological conditions (India, Sri Lanka, Bangladesh, Thailand, Vietnam and the Philippines). The government would assign counterparts on a permanent basis to work with the consulting group. (The mission learned that as many as 500 Laotian professional technicians had, during the past several years, been sent to Hanoi, Vietnam, for training and that they would soon be returning to Laos.) In addition, to the extent that sufficient counterparts could not be located, use would be made of *United Nations Volunteers* (similar to the Peace Corps of the U.S.).

The program was discussed and accepted by the Laotian authorities and the local UNDP officials. Officials of the Asian Development Bank and the World Bank, with whom the mission discussed the proposal, said that the concepts seemed good to them but they expressed reservations regarding implementation capacity even though the mission pointed out that Stage I would involve only studies and small wells, that it would be carried out independently under the direction of an expatriate consulting group and that the lack of implementation capacity presently impeding execution of conventional irrigation projects was therefore not a constraint in this case.

Monitoring the work of the consulting group would of course be essential and it would be desirable to maintain liaison with one of the international banks, either ADB or IBRD. IBRD seemed at the time more suitable because of its offices in Vientiane, which concentrated on procurement matters, and their regional office in Bangkok.

The mission observed that a small amount of water, available from one of the uncompleted dams, was being picked up by a temporary diversion weir to irrigate about 100 ha of land not previously cultivated. This land appeared to contain soils not suitable for rice cultivation; it was located in an area subject to flooding from the Nam Ngum River; and the average yield was only 700 kg per ha. At a closing meeting, the mission was told by the Acting Minister of Irrigation that the government intends to proceed with "provisional canals" to irrigate as much land as possible from the uncompleted dams. saying it was imperative to proceed in this way in view of the country's current rice shortage.

After its field work in Laos, the mission went to IFAD's headquarters in Rome to prepare its report which was issued June 1981 and forwarded to the government in March 1982.

In June 1982, while at the IFAD office in Rome in connection with another project, the author was asked to attend a meeting with IFAD officials and with A.M. Alam of the Agricultural Finance Corporation, Bombay, India. Alam had visited Laos and had prepared a draft report dated April 1982 disagreeing with the conclusions of the mission's June 1981 report and recommending a return to the FAO project of December 1980. Alam's arguments were mainly:

- There was no need to worry about the lack of hydrologic flow records since the Mekong Secretariat had made a "reliable estimate" based on analogy with some streams in Thailand.
- Water distribution and land leveling should not be a problem since the plan was to create farmers' cooperatives [My retort: Would these be collective farms *imposed* on the farmers?]
- He agreed that the feeder canals might leak but that "low-cost linings" could be devised.
- He agreed that the dams should be monitored by means of

piezometers.

- He accepted that groundwater investigations should proceed but should not hold up the implementation of a gravity-canal system.

A meeting at IFAD, Rome, on June 14, 1982 with Alam and the author present, supported the latter's position which was not to base the project on the two yet-to-be-completed dams and feeder canals but to proceed instead, as a next stage, with small-well development. But since the Laotian officials insisted on immediate use of the two dams and the feeder canals, without any desire to proceed with groundwater development and investigations, the net result was no project at all, at least for IFAD!

The author is not aware of what subsequently transpired.

This project illustrates several common failings to the approach often used in developing countries, especially the poorer ones such as Laos and several African countries; see the case of Mali in Chapter 5.

- Projects that involve massive and costly structures like dams have an allure and an appeal to many engineers, bureaucrats and politicians, a phenomenon known to development experts as *monumentalism*. Besides being a matter of national or personal pride, the large structures, unfortunately, often provide an opportunity for bribe-taking. That is *not* to say that all such structures are unjustified. Clearly the major dams controlling the Nile and the Narmada River in India (Chapters 2 and 8) *are* justified.
- The alternative to the large structures—and their *lumpy* investments—include small-scale facilities such as wells. These often have strong advantages.
- Whether large or small-scale facilities are the means adopted, much of the essential work of development is at the local level for which local leaders of adequate calibre or most often than not sadly lacking. Training and incentive-based programs are needed to overcome this deficiency. In the interim programs like UN Volunteers and the U.S. Peace Corps can help.
- Developing countries are often overrun by well-meaning (or self-seeking donors) who are in competition and do not act in a coordinated fashion. The attempts, such as those by the World Bank, to overcome this situation has not been very successful. See more in the final chapter.

Notes

1. M.A. Ghani et al "Gravity Irrigation Management in Bangladesh" *J., Irrigation and Drainage Engrg.*, ASCE Aug 1989, 115 (642-655).

3. Peter Rogers et al, "Water Development in Bangladesh: A Retrospective on the Flood Action Plan," 1994, Synthesis Report prepared for the Bureau for Asia and the Near East of the U.S. Agency for International Development by the Irrigation Support Project for Asia and the Near East, 18..

4. World Bank, Asia Region, Country Department I, "Bangladesh: Action Plan for Flood Control," 1989..

5. N. N. Bhattachrya and A. K. Bora, "Floods of The Brahmaputra River in India," 1997, *Water International*, Vol. 22, 222-229.

6. L. Douglas James. "Flood Action: An Opportunity for Bangladesh," 1994, *Water International*, Vol. 19, 61-69. Phillip Kirpich, Letter to the Editor (comment on James' article), 1995, *Water International*, Vol. 20, 53.

7. World Bank "Project Completion Report, Chandpur II Irrigation Project," August 22, 1980.

8. IFAD "Small-Scale Flood Control, Drainage and Irrigation Project," October 1982.

9. H. Brammer, "Agriculture and Food Production in Polder Areas: A Case Story from Bangladesh," *Water International,* Vol. 8, 74-81. Phillip Kirpich, Letter to the Editor (comment on Brammer's article), 1994, *Water International,* Vol. 9, 42.

10. F.E. Schulze, Robert Chambers and Phillip Kirpich, "Report of the Study Team on Water Management Research and Training," 1982, CGIAR, Technical Advisory Committee, Rome.

11 "Where India's Reforms get stuck," *The Economist*, January 22, 1994.

12. Robert Wade, "The System of Administrative and Political Corruption: Canal Irrigation in South India," 1982, *The Journal of Development Studies*, Vol. 18, No. 3, 286-328.

13. Harald D. Frederiksen "Water Crisis in Developing World: Misconceptions about Solutions," *J. Water Resources Planning and Management*, ASCE, 1996, 122(2), 79-87. Discussion: Phillip Z. Kirpich, 1997, *J. Water Resources Planning and Management*, ASCE, Sept-Oct 1997, 314-315.

Chapter 4

LESSONS FROM PAST CASES, NORTH AFRICA

The situations in two of the three Maghreb (from Arabic meaning northwest Africa) countries—Morocco and Tunisia—are discussed here, which leaves out Algeria. Egypt and Sudan are discussed in Chapter 8 on the Middle East.

Morocco

Population in 1997: 28,200,000	Population growth rate: 2.0%
Population in 2025: 39,900,000	Area: 626,000 km^2
Fertility rate: 3.3	Life expectancy: 68 years
Per capita GNP (US$): 1,110	Percent urban: 51

Morocco, like Tunisia, offers exotic scenery and has a fascinating history. The country was a French/Spanish protectorate from 1912 to 1956. Spain's presence was in the small and relatively humid Mediterranean coastal zone, while France dominated the rest of the country which is arid to semi-arid. The French influence has continued, particularly with respect to irrigated agriculture.

Two visits were made to Morocco, both for the World Bank. The first, for three weeks in 1962, was for appraisal of a loan for an agricultural project involving improvements for irrigation and for animal husbandry. The second, in 1967, with a duration of two months, was for review of all agricultural projects and programs in the country; these were universally oriented toward irrigated agriculture. The mission was composed of an agriculturist (mission leader), an agricultural economist, a credit specialist and an irrigation engineer.

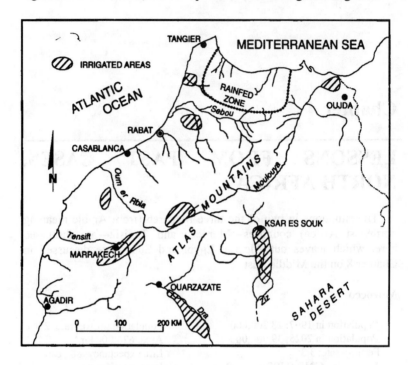

Fig. 4-1. Irrigation Perimeters in Morocco

The 1967 mission was asked to provide a preliminary judgement on eleven projects, all involving large dams, plus two long-range studies of two river basins, the Sebou and the Oum Er R'bia. Since the projects and studies were located throughout the country, a unique opportunity was provided to get a comprehensive view of the entire agricultural sector of the economy.

The mission's findings, which were set forth in a two-volume report,[1] did not find favor with leading Moroccan officials—a reaction that had been foretold during closing discussions held prior to the mission's departure. Here is a summary of the report's conclusions, with most of which the officials disagreed:0

- The Government's main effort during the past decade has been in large, high-cost irrigation projects (Fig. 4-1) whose justification is in doubt owing to high construction costs and delays in implementation. Only 4,000 ha were developed over the past 10 to 12 years and with the continued high costs, the government's proposed program to develop 25,000 ha of new irrigation annually is neither realistic nor economically desirable.

- More attention should be paid to the extensive rainfed zone where the annual rainfall exceeds 450 mm and where there is a large potential for cultivation of cereals. Overcoming the prevailing constraints in the rainfed zone—land-tenure adjustments and provision of credit to small farmers—is admittedly a painful task to execute in a political sense, but is nevertheless essential.

- Like rainfed cereals, livestock production has received insufficient attention, despite the country's vast extent of suitable rangelands. This, again, is a politically difficult problem that has to be addressed. In the 7,800,000 ha of rangeland in the country, the key problem is *overgrazing,* which to solve will require a combination of persuasion and policing..

- With respect to individual irrigation projects, rather than embarking on new irrigation projects, the emphasis should be on completion and improvement of projects for which large capital investments have already been made and which cover an aggregate area of about 150,000 ha.

- Capital investments for new irrigation projects need rigorous investigation of economic and social factors. While use of the high-technology *canaux portés* system developed in France (see below) has its advantages, it also has disadvantages (including high cost and its continued use should be reexamined. Manpower constraints indicate that the rate of development should not exceed 7,000 ha per year.

- Three large dams—Ait-Adel, Ziz and Draa—are not justified and should not proceed. These three cases provide graphic illustrations of the facile thinking, prevalent in many countries, whereby large *lumpy investments,* such as for large dams, are considered to be panaceas that 0can cure all ills. For further description of these three cases, see below under "Monumental Dams."

- The organizations operating the irrigation projects need improvement in staff qualifications and in procedures for

collection of water charges.
- The limited increase in agricultural production obtainable by irrigation does not mean that investment in large-scale irrigation should be abandoned, particularly in the Rharb plain in the Sebou basin and the Tadla region in the Oum Er R'bai basin where benefits from hydroelectricity can mitigate the high cost of the irrigation infrastructure.
- Aside from channeling of capital investments, key policy questions that need resolution, if substantially increased agricultural production is to be realized, include <u>land-tenure arrangements</u> (already mentioned), <u>nationalization of foreign-held land</u>, and promotion of <u>cooperative farming</u>, as a means of assisting the great number of farmers with small landholdings. Government policy—and leadership—will also be needed for essential efforts related to <u>agricultural credit and marketing</u> and <u>agricultural extension</u>.

The conclusions and recommendations set forth in the review of 1967 represented a tall order for the Government, probably well in excess of its capability to execute. The mission's report contained warnings and made constructive suggestions regarding directions that the Government should take in trying to stimulate much needed increases in agricultural production.

However, little happened in subsequent years. Old ways of doing things persist for a long time. It is most likely that the situation in Morocco with respect to irrigated agriculture is little different today from what it was thirty years ago. The key indicators given above regarding the current population growth rate and GNP per capita bear this out. *The Economist* in its issue of June 7, 1997 stated:

> Roughly half of Moroccan adults cannot read or write. The universities are still turning out would-be bureaucrats, not business-minded graduates. Mass illiteracy and high graduate unemployment hinder the development of the broad middle class that is an economic motor in other emerging markets.

The World Bank's management endorsed the findings of the 1967 mission but whether a significant follow-up took place seems doubtful.

Large Dams

Love for large dams is a worldwide phenomenon and Morocco is no exception. Politicians love large dams because they serve as monuments that can bear their names, or, the dams provide almost ideal opportunities for bribes paid by eager design and construction contractors.

As for the function of large dams, the underlying principle is simple: Store wet-season excesses—while reducing flood damages—and use the stored water in the dry season. Two drawbacks with respect to this simplistic thinking are: First, much more than just building a dam is required. For a development involving irrigation, a distribution system has to be planned, constructed (often in stages), implemented and maintained. The users—typically illiterate peasants with very small landholdings—have to be organized and assisted in many ways.

Second, as often claimed by environmentalists, the *negative* benefits from a particular dam have to be considered such as resettlement of the displaced population, loss of habitat for animal and plant life and damage to archeological treasures. Of course, when the positive benefits clearly exceed the negative ones—which I believe to be so in the case of the Assuan dam in Egypt and of the Sardar Sarovar dam in India (see Chapters 3 and 8)—construction of the dam in question should by all means proceed.

Another problem with dams is that they trap sediments and thus gradually lose their original storage capacity. This tends to be more serious for watersheds with little or poor vegetative or forest cover as in arid climates or where the inhabitants, needing fuel for cooking or for warmth, have stripped the forests.

The 1967 mission acknowledged that several of the large dams constructed earlier may have been justified, but not several of those then proposed, with particular reference to the three mentioned above: Ait-Adel, Ziz and Draa.

The Ait-Adel Dam

This dam was proposed as a means of increasing the extent of irrigated land in the Tessaout-Amont plain near Marrakech. Studies carried out by the French agency SCET-Cooperation included land-classification studies indicating that of the 63,700 ha in the plain, 48,000 ha were suitable for irrigation, either intensively (for tree crops, beans or corn, sometimes mixed with cereals) or semi-intensively (for cereals only); however, only 6,000 ha were considered to be of first-class quality. SCET also determined that most of the area was already irrigated, although much of it using primitive methods, with the following breakdown (in ha):

Traditional (watercourses drawing water by means
   f primitive intakes)   9,000
Pumping from groundwater   4,800
Mixed traditional and pumping   3,600
Non-irrigated   5,700
Total   63,700

The 1967 mission found that a project for intensive irrigation of Tessaout-Amont, if based on the Ait Aidel dam, would be excessively costly as compared with the benefits likely to be obtained. The additional water from the dam would enable an increase of only 7,000 ha above the 6,000 ha already intensively irrigated from the natural, unregulated flow of the Oued Tessaout dam. The mission proposed instead (a) that this flow be utilized to upgrade and intensify the 11,000-ha traditional system and to develop an additional 10,000 ha on a non-intensive basis, and (b) that use be made of groundwater combined with available surface water for intensive irrigation in the northern portion of the plain.

The mission felt and stated, that, owing to its high cost, the Ait Aidel dam should not be built and that the money saved should be used for development in more promising areas.

The Draa and Ziz Dams

The *wadis* (dry river beds) in the Draa and Ziz valleys in south-central Morocco, each with a length of about 200 km, discharge flash floods of short duration during the winter months. Originating from rainfall and snowmelt from the southeastern slopes of the Atlas Mountains, the floods diminish gradually in a downstream direction and finally disappear into the Sahara Desert.

The Draa Valley begins at the village of Agdz and stretches southeasterly for about 200 km to the village of Mhamid. Agdz is 75 km from Ouarzazate, the main town in the region, but with a population of only 2,000. Ouarzazate is connected by a good road to Marrakech. From Agdz to Mhami, there is a passable dirt road. Mhami is at the end of the road. To proceed further into the Sahara, one must follow camel trails.

Local farmers have for centuries made use of the flash floods, through a practice known as *spate irrigation.*[2] Waters from the flash floods are diverted from streams or rivers by primitive works. Even though the floods are of short duration, the farmers are able to douse their lands sufficiently enough so that moisture retained in the soils is enough to grow a subsistence crop.

The Draa Valley consists of a series of *palmeraies* (groupings of date palms) all of which are long and narrow, the width varying from 1 to 2 km. In 1967, there were seven such palmeraies, with a total cultivated area of about 20,000 ha and a population of 110,000. Crops grown, mainly for subsistence, were dates, barley and wheat, all entirely dependent on irrigation, either from the Oued Draa (mainly by means of the primitive, traditional intakes) or from groundwater, the use of which had been increasing.

The mission was told that fifty years earlier there had been five million date palms in the valley but that owing to disease only a million were left. Nevertheless, date production continues to be a mainstay of the basically subsistence economy, with half going into auto-consumption and half for export elsewhere in Morocco. Improved marketing of dates was a goal that the government was planning to do something about.

Study of a possible storage dam at a site "Zaouia N'Ourbaz" was begun July 1966 by the firm Hydroproyect of the USSR. Concurrently, the French firm Soletranche began subsurface explorations for the dam. Negotiations were underway with a Yugoslav firm for studies of a system for distribution of irrigation water in the area downstream of the dam. The lake formed by the dam would cover 5,000 ha of which 600 ha are presently cultivated.

The upstream farmers in the Draa Valley had prior rights to the available water, while those downstream, under the system of spate irrigation being followed, had only the surplus. In years when the winter floods were less than normal; the surplus was less but it was at least something. The mission pointed out that, following completion of the dam, flash flooding would be eliminated entirely, which would mean that except for farmers near the dam and served by a distribution system leading from the dam, downstream farmers would get nothing at all!

With the valley's farmers accustomed over the centuries to *spate irrigation*, might it not be better to leave the physical conditions more or less as they were? Or perhaps thought could be given to replacing some of the primitive diversion works with permanent ones not subject to washout every year.

In the valley of the Ziz, although there is no shortage of land with soils of good quality, water rather than land determines the extent of cultivation. Water comes from three sources: *rhettaras*, which are underground galleries similar to the *ghanats* of the Middle East, 1,600 ha; groundwater pumping, 500 ha; and surface water diverted by primitive means from the Oued Ziz and one of its tributaries, which varies from 4,500 ha to as much as 14,500 ha—another instance of *spate irrigation.*

The population of 120,000 depends on subsistence cropping, limited to cereals, alfalfa, dates and a few pulses. None of the agricultural production is exported out of the region. The average landholding is less than a hectare and is moreover divided into as many as ten plots. Each plot is protected by earth walls 2 to 2.5 m high serving as windbreaks. With the small plots and high population density the type of agriculture practiced may rather be called "gardening". The three elements—land, water and people—are in equilibrium. The average caloric intake per person is about 1,800, which is not below the average for Morocco. There is some exodus of population to maintain this balance.

Many studies had been carried out by agencies of the National Government. One of the recent studies had been assisted by a Yugoslav team and the mission learned that the team's work would be extended to cover *"petites hydrauliques"* including improvement of the rhettaras to reduce leakage, water-spreading to further increase the flow to the rhettaras and additional pumped wells to further exploit groundwater. It was estimated that these works and improvements would enable increase in the area irrigated from these sources from 6,300 ha to 10,300 ha.

A major flood in 1965 gave impetus to the idea of constructing a major storage dam on the Oued Ziz. TAMS, a U.S. engineering firm, was engaged for a preliminary study and in October 1966 recommended a site at Foum Rhior.

The mission however concluded that the additional water obtainable from Foum Rhior would enable irrigation of only 2,300 ha on a "perennial" basis and 1,800 ha on a "semiperennial" basis, which would be too little to justify the dam. Flood control benefits would likewise be too small to affect justification. A further major disadvantage of the dam would be that, as in the case of the Draa Valley, it would do away with the spate-irrigation system being depended upon by most of the farmers in the 200-km-long valley.

From former colleagues employed by TAMS, by whom the author had been employed from 1947 to 1962, he learned that the Foum Rhior dam was completed in 1971. He was not however able to determine the extent to which the dire consequences foretold by the 1967 mission took place.

A High-Tech Water Distribution System—Justified?

The mission thought that, besides the dams, another reason for the high current cost of irrigation in Morocco was the elaborate nature of the irrigation-water distribution system. This system was based almost exclusively on the use of *canaux portés* (elevated above-ground canals) for secondary and tertiary canals, the latter generally on a spacing of 100 m. The *canaux portés* are made up of concrete elements, either semicircular or parabolic, that are precast and prestressed in fabrication plants of which there were four in the country. Following transport from the factory, the elements are mounted on concrete pedestals. Joints consist of rubber gaskets. Road and other crossings are accomplished by means of inverted siphons; although expensive, this is the only practicable method of crossing the precast canals, as ramping over them, as for earth canals, would not be feasible. In addition, ingenious automatic devices, called *modules à masques*, are provided for control and measurement of water flows. Although easy to operate, these have the disadvantage of causing a head loss which, in the case of the secondaries, can amount to as much as 0.4 m. Another disadavantage of the *canaux portés* system is that the rather light, precast concrete elements are vulnerable to damage from vehicles or agricultural machinery. Except for Tunisia, Turkey and to a limited extent Greece, the system has not had widespread use.

The question of *appropriate technology,* an important one for the developing countries, has aroused controversy in recent decades. Some practitioners, as in a publication authored by three World Bank staff members,[3] favor rapid modernization using up-to-date, sophisticated technology. Others, including the author, have a preference for technology that is not over-sophisticated, with greater emphasis given to eliminating deficiencies in management and related institutional problems. Caution needs to be exercised in introducing high technology—a view shared by another World Bank staff member[4] and by three experts from Israel[5] where the level of sophistication is among the highest in the world. The use of high technology has proved disappointing in many developing countries; concurrently the realization has grown that correcting deficiencies in management and related institutional problems has become urgent. This view was expressed in a 1997 review of literature dealing with water user associations (WUAs);[6] see also quotation in Chapter 1 from a keynote address by John Hennessy, former President of ICID.

Tunisia

Population in 1997: 9,300,000	Population growth rate: 1.9%
Population in 2025: 13,500,000	Area: 125,580 km^2
Fertility rate: 3.3	Life expectancy: 68 years
Per capita GNP (US$): 1,820	Percent urban: 58

Tunisia's water-management problems are serious, more so than Morocco's. Although the range of climatic conditions are similar, Tunisia lacks sizeable rivers that drain a mountainous mass, as do the rivers in Morocco. Tourism based on famous antiquities and exotic beaches is an important asset that Tunisia exploits. But this asset is now threatened by increasing pollution, both from sources within the country and from the other countries that border the Mediterranean Sea.

Tunisia suffers from several other environmental problems including soil erosion, desertification, deterioration of rangelands, and loss of forest cover and wetlands. In its irrigated zones there are dangers from salinization and from pollution that threaten groundwater aquifers. The government has been well aware of these dangers and has begun steps to curb them. Concurrently, the World Bank had since the late 1970s become increasingly concerned with threats to the environment and therefore to sustainable development. Becoming involved with Tunisia's environmental problems appeared attractive to the Bank because of the government's demonstrated interest and commitment to deal with these problems. Moreover, the Bank, through

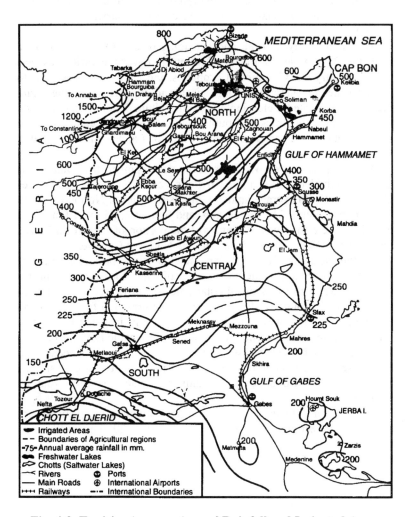

Fig. 4-2. Tunisia: Average Annual Rainfall and Irrigated Areas

past loans to Tunisia, had developed high regard for the Tunisian staff
assigned. Here was an excellent opportunity to hold the country up as
an example to the many other developing countries with similar
problems.

Beginning early in 1988 and extending over a period of almost a
year, the Bank assigned a team of twenty to cover the various aspects
of the country's environmental problems. the author was assigned to
handle water resources but with liaison and support from other team
members in related fields including agriculture, public health, waste
management, economics and public administration. A comprehensive
report containing a series of recommendations appeared in December
1988.

For the planning of water resources development, the country has
been subdivided into three regions called "Water Resources
Complexes," with average annual rainfalls as follows: Northern, 350 to
1,500 mm; Central, 210 to 350 mm; and Southern, 75 to 210 mm; see
Fig. 4-2. There follows a summary of the portion of the World Bank's
December 1988 report that deals with the Northern Complex.[7]

In the Northern Complex, the Mejerda River basin has primary
importance because it is the main source of water for irrigation and for
supply of water to the major coastal cities, from Bizerte and Tunis in
the north as far south as Sfax in the south. At present, of the 93,000 ha
"equipped" for irrigation, 80,000 ha are actually irrigated but only a
third is double-cropped. The area ultimately attainable is about 100,000
ha, which if double-cropped would produce gross values exceeding that
of the rest of the country. Given Tunisia's food-trade gap and its
vulnerability to droughts, it is highly important that this goal be
achieved.

But there are difficulties owing largely to conflicting demands for
scarce water, estimated as follows for the year 2010 in millions of
m³/yr:

Irrigation		590
Municipal		
Tunis area	261	
Bizerte area	31	
Export to South	<u>22</u>	423
Industrial		<u>100</u>
TOTAL		1,113

The water available *in an average year* is 1,461million m³ from surface sources and 35 million m³ from groundwater. In a *drought year* (defined as occuring in one out of five years for irrigation and in one out of ten years for municipal and industrial), the studies indicated that the demand could still be met, provided that *contingency plans* have been prepared to deal with such emergencies.

In preparing contingency plans for the Northern Complex, consideration has to be given not just to a one-in-five or a one-in-ten dry year but also to a *sequence* of dry years as has occured several times since rainfall records have been kept (since 1938). As the Northern Complex has many storage reservoirs, sequences of dry years are more significant than single dry years.

Despite the apparently adequate quantity of water in an average year, it would be wrong to become complacent in view of the following series of unfavorable factors that have still to be overcome:

- Loss of storage in the reservoirs due to sediments from soil erosion
- Eutrophication of the reservoirs (mainly from agricultural wastes) resulting in deterioration of water quality and therefore of the quantity available
- Salinization of irrigated lands requiring additional water for leaching
- Damage to groundwater aquifers from agricultural and industrial wastes
- Added water needed for preservation of wetlands, especially Lac Ishkeul
- A further uncertainty results from the fact that the estimate of future demand of water for irrigation has assumed high efficiency in its use which has still to be realized in practice. Water Users Associations (Associations d'Intérêt Collectif or AICs) were established by law in 1987 but rules for allocation of charges to individual farmer-members had not been owrked out. Also pending were decisions on the extent of physical improvements needed including measuring devices and land leveling, and on use of treated sewage for iirrigation of cotton and tree crops (but not for vegetables).

Use of high-tech such as drip irrigation (for tree crops and vegetables) is another means of conserving water; however, its adoption would depend on farmers' willingness and ability to bear the cost. As the 1988 report states, it would seem necessary as a prerequisite to engage in a sustained effort to make the AICs effective.

To achieve improved efficiency of irrigation while overcoming the five unfavorable factors mentioned, will require continued and strenuous efforts by the Tunisian authorities. These authorities do realize that such efforts are indeed needed to avert what could be a serious water crisis. In view of what these authorities have actually accomplished, one can be hopeful that the necessary actions will be accomplished in time.

Lac Ishkeul is a 9,000 ha body of water that has excited interest among conservationists worldwide owing to its major importance as a refuge and breeding area for migratory waterfowl. On a mountain on the south shore of the lake, a museum devoted to waterfowl has proved to be attractive for conservations, tourists and others interested in observing the migratory waterfowl. But the lake is directly affected by several dams, either already built or proposed, and by wastes from irrigated areas that drain into the lake. A study was underway to reduce the area of the lake by about a third so as to reduce the large evaporation losses that occur during the dry season, thereby increasing the supply of water for irrigation and for municipal use; the lake would however be preserved for fish breeding and as a waterfowl refuge. The lake had caused and was continuing to cause heated controversy between ecologists and others desiring more water for municipal use. The Bank's December 1988 report advised compromise based on an adequate public discussion of the issues.

The Bank's report contained many recommendations, some of them quite detailed, concerning future management of land and water resources. Probably, the most difficult actions to accomplish will be of an administrative nature, considering that as many as twelve separate government agencies are involved. It will take political will and leadership to designate the lead gency for each major task and to take steps to achieve overall coordination.

Notes

1. World Bank, Projects Department, "Review of Agricultural Projects and Programs, Morocco," Report No. TO-604, September 13, 1967.

2. W. A. Van Tuijl, "Improved Spate Irrigation" in World Bank Technical Paper Number 94 "Technological and Institutional Innovation in Irrigation," 1989, 13.

3. Hervé Plusquellec et al, "Modern Water Control in Irrigation; Concepts, Issues and Applications," World Bank Technical Paper Number 246, 1994.

4. W. A. Van Tuijl, "Improving Water Use in Agriculture; Experiences in the Middle East and North Africa," World bank Technical Paper Number 201, 1993.

5. April 1989 "Technological and Institutional Innovation in Irrigation" World Bank Technical Paper No. 94. David Melamed "Technological Developments: the Israeli Experience," 23-36; Meir Ben-Meir "Establishing Research Prioities," 108-112; Moshe Sne "the Role of Extension in Irrigation," 116-127.

6. April 1997 "User Organizations for Sustainable Water Services," World Bank Technical Paper No. 354, page 18.

7. World Bank, "Tunisia, Country Environmental Study, Supporting Report No. 3, The Degradation of Land and Water Resources," December 1988, 33-72.

Chapter 5

LESSONS FROM PAST CASES, SUB-SAHARAN AFRICA

Poverty in Sub-Saharan Africa is severe with half the population below the poverty line. Agriculture, the primary source of food and by far the main source of employment, has not performed well in the 1980s and 1990s despite widespread activities of international donors.[12]

Ivory Coast

Population in 1997: 15,000,000   Population growth rate: 2.6%
Population in 2025: 26,500,000   Area: 322,463 km^2
Fertility rate: 5.7   Life expectancy: 51 years
Per capita GNP (US$): 660   Percent urban: 46

The story of the Kossou Dam is of interest as it illustrates three obstacles to efficient water management for the benefit of developing countries: *monumentalism, unethical conduct* (by contractors) and *lack of coordination among international agencies* (to coordinate policies).

The Kossou Dam is on the Bandama River, which is the most centrally located of the five main rivers of the country (Fig. 5-1) Near the dam is Yamousoukro, the capital and hometown of Félix Houphouët-Boigny, President of the country from 1960—the year of independence from France—until the present. The country's main city, A0bidjan, is on the coast, 250 km away.

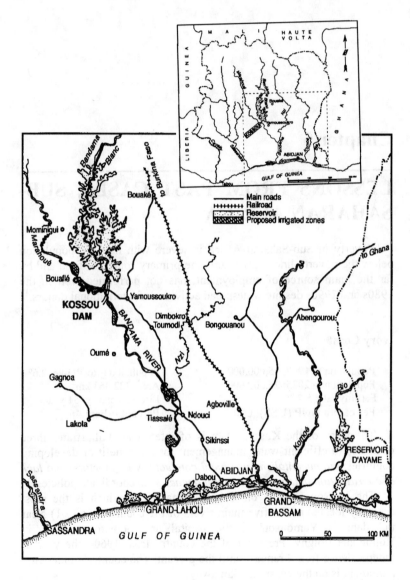

Fig. 5-1. Ivory Coast: Bandama Project and Kossou Dam

The President very much wanted the dam and had engaged two prominent international consulting firmss to prepare the necessary designs and feasibility reports: Electricité de France, and Kaiser Engineers and Constructors of U.S.A

In October 1964, a report on the Bandama river Project, which included the Kossou Dam, was presented to the World Bank. The Bank's review, which was limited to the electric-power aspects of the project and was completed February 1965, concluded that the project would not be justified for hydroelectric power, mainly because an alternative thermal-electric plant would be much more economic. The Government and its consultants countered by claiming that additional *agricultural* benefits would accrue that would make the project justifiable.

Kaiser Engineers, one of the consultants, prepared another report dated August 1965 setting forth these claims and transmitted it to the Bank. The author was asked to head a mission to the Ivory Coast to check on Kaiser's contention that the additional benefits resulting from irrigation would make the project justifiable.. While organizing the mission, information available in Washington concerning land suitability and rainfall was examined, leading to a conclusion that irrigation could not be justified as a benefit from the Bandama dam. Little suitable land was available and there was ample rainfall for the small area that was suitable. Therefore, the mission would really be a waste of time.

However, there were political considerations to take into account. The Ivory Coast being *francophone* and the Bank having often been accused of being anti-francophone, it was decided to try to please the Ivorians and to proceed with the mission. Besides the author as leader, the mission included an agricultural economist, a soils expert and experts on tropical crops including sugarcane and pineapples.

In Abidjan, then the capital of the Ivory Coast, the mission soon met President Houphouet-Boigny. He drove the author in his open car through Yamasoukro, where he was loudly cheered by the locals. The mission was invited to spend the night at his luxurious villa on a small lake nearby where he kept pet alligators.

The President told the mission that if it needed help from the consultants, he would gladly arrange to bring them from California. The mission's reply was no, that it had all the needed information. However, two days later a team from Kaiser appeared. The mission leader told the team leader that it would call on them if needed.

Although the mission made no such call, two days later the team came anyhow and commenced to put the mission under pressure pointing to the   importance of this project to the country, and to enduring friendship between the U.S. and the Ivory Coast. The mission replied that it would take all this under advisement but that a decision would have to await its return to Washington. This response was not a heated one except for the mission's economist who lost his cool in the face of the consultants' pressure, calling them "lackeys" and "hucksters."

The consultants repeated past arguments that the growing of pineapples could be appropriate on a big scale from water provided by the dam. But the mission was not able to agree in view of the limited land and ample rainfall. Upon return to Washington, the mission painstakingly wrote its report[3] which was translated into French so that it could be sent to the Ivorians and to the French Executive Director (a World Bank Board member) so as to demonstrate that the Bank was acting for the good of both the Ivory Coast and the Bank and without prejudice against any francophone country.

The Kaiser team returned to California to report what it considered a disappointing result. It must also have reported the abusive language used by the mission's economist. Word was soon received that this person was being asked to resign by the Bank's Personnel Department. Despite efforts by the mission members to defend him—saying, yes, he had lost his cool but then the consultants had been very provocative— he had to resign.

These events did not however put the Bandama Dam project to rest. Three years later, for apparently *purely political reasons* but maybe also because of Kaiser's influence in Washington, the project was financed by the Export-Import Bank, an agency of the U.S. Government.

Mali

Population in 1997: 9,900,000	Population growth rate: 3.0%
Population in 2025: 23,700,000	Area: 1,240,000 km^2
Fertility rate: 6.7	Life expectancy: 44 years
Per capita GNP (US$): 250	Percent urban: 26

This case illustrates three factors that often inhibit sound development in low-income countries: failure to consult with and get ideas from the local population, reluctance of bureaucrats to spend time in rural villages away from the capital city, and resistance by international agencies to innovation even when old methods have not worked.

Mali is a West African country, a large part of which lies in the Sahel. The Sahel, a semi-arid belt crossing Africa south of the Sahara, frequently suffers famines caused by droughts. A UNDP/UNICEF project, underway since 1976, had centered in the Kolokani Cercle, a 10,500 km^2 civil subdivision representative of the Plateau Mandingue, which covers 70,000 km^2 in the Sahel. Out of 239 villages in Kolokani, 118 had been provided (by mid-1984) with potable water for "basic human needs," set at 30 liters/day/capita. Similar efforts in other parts of the plateau were being financed by other donors.

With a population of 97,300 and density of 9.3/km^2, the Cercle was thinly populated. The population of the villages then served varied from 47 to 2,785 with an average of 450. Village, hand-dug wells provided water for domestic use and livestock and to a very limited extent for small vegetable gardens but were unsanitary and unreliable during drought conditions. Under the project, drilled wells were installed, depth 40 to 70 m, static lift 10 to 25 m, each equipped with a handpump of generally 1 m^3/hr capacity. Improved handpumps, recently developed and fabricated locally, pumped 1 to 2 m^3/hr for static lifts of less than 15 m, which occurred in about half of the wells.

Then a breakthrough occurred. The villagers found that there was some excess of water beyond their per capita need of 30 liters/day and they began using this excess to increase the areas and yields of their garden plots, even though it meant back-breaking hand-carry from the wells to the plots. In 1984, the author was engaged by the UNDP to determine if there was merit in expanding the program of well drilling and use of handpumps so as to gain this unexpected benefit from gardening. He spent two weeks in the villages and held meetings with the villagers and their headmen. The universal cry was for more water. They said the increase in gardening would not only give them a better diet; it would also produce revenue since they could sell some of the produce in nearby market towns. Before expanding the wells and handpump program, there were some questions to be answered:

- What quantity of groundwater can be relied upon? From another UNDP program, it was learned that there was enough in the Kolokani Cercle for as much as 52,500 ha.
- Should small motorized pumps be considered instead of handpumps

since the capacity of the drilled wells averaged 5 m³/hr, or 2 to 5 times the handpump capacity?

- When substantially more water becomes available for the garden plots, how should the villagers organize themselves to make use of it? How would the produce—tomatoes, onions, tobacco and potatoes—be marketed?
- Can water from the wells be used as well for *wet-season crops* (for millet, the main subsistence crop, and for maize for animal fodder) as supplemental irrigation when the rains fail or are skimpy as often happens? (The villagers said, yes, by all means.)
- Who would operate the motor pumps and how would the costs be recovered?

The author's preliminary investigations indicated that use of motorized pumps would indeed be favorable. Each pump would have a capacity of about 6 m³/hr (about 25 gallons per minute) against a static lift of 25 m maximum. The motors, either diesel, gasoline or kerosene, would be of about ¾ horsepower. The cost was estimated at $1,400 per motorpump. Owing to their small size (about 1½-inch discharge pipe), handling and installing of the pumps and motors should present no problem.

Maintenance of the motorpumps would require recruiting and training local staff to operate and maintain the pumps. For the 239 villages in the Kolkani Cercle, about 50 operators would need to be trained, assuming one operator per 5 motorpumps. The motorpumps are simple pieces of equipment, far less complex than trucks and agricultural equipment that Malians are well able to service and maintain.

The author recommended that as a next step a Demonstration cum Research Project be carried out. Concurrently, an elementary feasibility study would be prepared for each village including layout of enlarged garden plots, with water distribution probably by hoses; determination of fertilizer sources, particularly animal manure; and marketing arrangements. Despite the differences, mainly physical, among the villages, the scope of the feasibility studies would be similar. After a few studies had been completed, the carrying out of additional ones would become easier and less time consuming.

Owing to the large number of villages, the feasibility studies would have to be carried out by Malian staff with only limited foreign help. Innovative thinking on the related questions of training and people-management would be needed using known technologies. Although not easy, the effort would be well justified in view of the great need and wide applicability in the Sahel and considering that *the large-scale capital-intensive projects (e.g., in Nigeria and Mali), are greatly underutilized.* (They were carried out with almost no consideration of the foregoing village-level factors.) That international donors have failed to appreciate the primary role of *small-scale vs. large-scale development* has been well expressed by a leading African agricultural economist.[4]

Even though the government and UNDP officials found the author's ideas interesting, no action was taken. The author's surmise is that these officials were discouraged by the relatively long times required for the feasibility studies and the admittedly tricky task of finding Malian staff to carry them out. Since no other viable alternative for many zones in the Sahel that are similar to Kolokani is available, it is the author's opinion that the approach he has recommended should be tried out with little delay.

Notes

1. IFPRI, "A 2020 Vision for Food, Agriculture and the Environment in Sub-Saharan Africa," Discussion Paper 4, June 1995.

2. World Bank, "Ivory Coast. Appraisal of the Agricultural Aspects of Proposed Bandama River Project," Report No.T O-521, February 1966.

3. Mandivamba Rukuni, "Getting Agriculture Moving in Eastern and Southern Africa and a Framework for Action," IFPRI, *op. cit.,* 36-54.

Chapter 6

LESSONS FROM PAST CASES, LATIN AMERICA

The *Interamerican Dialogue on Water Management*, held in Miami October 27-30, 1993, brought nearly 450 delegates from nineteen countries. The Proceedings of the Dialogue[1] states that the meeting had two main objectives. One was to <u>increase awareness and understanding of the importance of sustainable development and integrated water-resource management</u>. The second was <u>establishing an Interamerican Water Resource Network</u>. A second Dialogue took place in Buenos Aires in September 1996 and a third is planned to take place in Central America in 1999.

These meetings have been useful for interchange of information and experiences so as to benefit from both achievements and mistakes made in the past. Florida was chosen as the venue for the first meeting because, resulting from the pressure of rapid population growth, Florida has done much pioneering in water resource development, embracing not just technological questions but social, economic and political ones as well. A second reason was the initiative taken by one of the leading Florida State agencies concerned: the South Florida Water Management District (SFWMD), which, in terms the population affected and the size of its staff, is the largest of five such districts that cover the entire State. SFWMD over the past several decades has had many successes (and some failures) that attracted attention throughout Latin America, and felt it was time to share some of its knowledge and experience with its Latin American neighbors to the south.

In order to advance beyond the discussion stage it was also proposed to find more definite linkages, one in particular: the *Pantanal* of Brazil and the *Everglades* of Florida.[2] Both comprise very large wetlands subject to severe environmental hazards. The Everglades are of vital interest to the urban conglomerations nearby, as a primary source of water supply but also as a means of maintaining the purity and soundness of coastal waters. The Pantanal covers a vast area of perhaps as much as 40,000,000 ha. The *original* area of the Everglades was about 1,600,000 ha, but half of that has given way to urban, industrial and agricultural development. Development of the Pantanal, in contrast, is in its infancy. But that condition will not last and it is indeed wise for the Brazilian, Paraguayan and Bolivian governments to take steps so that development of the Pantanal can proceed on a sound basis. For further discussion of the Pantanal, see below under Brazil.

As start of significant development of the Pantanal is probably a long way off, the question arises as to whether there are other regions in Latin America where problems are more urgent and need earlier attention. To address this question, the author prepared a paper that was presented at the Dialogue in Miami.[3] The paper lists eight regions that should have priority, chosen on the basis of positive answers to the following three questions:

- Does the region contain a large population as compared with other regions?
- Is water management critical to sustainable development of the region?
- Is it feasible to achieve substantial progress toward sustainable development in the medium term (10 to 20 years)?

The eight regions thus selected were: MEXICO, the Gulf Coast; BRAZIL, the Northeast; ECUADOR, the Lower Guayas Valley; PERU, the Coast; COLOMBIA, the Upper Cauca Valley; COLOMBIA, the Lower Cauca/Magdalena Valleys; and CHILE, the Santiago Region. Herein two more have been added: HAITI, the Artibonite Valley; and the DOMINICAN REPUBLIC making a total of ten. Although there are many who will dispute these choices, the fact remains that the making of choices is important if adequate progress is to be achieved in a reasonable time, especially for the urgent cases. This chapter contains descriptions of the ten regions.

Mexico

Population in 1997: 95,700,000	Population growth rate: 2.2%
Population in 2025: 140,800,000	Area: 1,981,000 km^2
Fertility rate: 3.1	Life expectancy: 72 years
Per capita GNP (US$): 3,320	Percent urban: 71

Mexico's achievement in irrigation of its arid and semi-arid regions—over 5 million ha under irrigation—is impressive and it has programs for improving the yields and efficiency of water use in these regions.[4] These programs are vital in order to grow more food for an increasing population and to gain foreign currency from export of high-value vegetables and fruits, mainly under irrigation.

Under NAFTA, the U.S. market for Mexican vegetables and fruits should be virtually unlimited. Increased trade in these items would bring many benefits: to both the Mexican and the U.S. economies.

- Mexico would be better able to buy more U.S. industrial goods, and agricultural commodities too, like corn which in the U.S. is produced in massive industrial-type operations. In Mexico, corn should be replaced by labor-intensive crops like vegetables and fruits.
- The increase in Mexican demand for U.S. products would create jobs in the U.S.
- Increased income for Mexican campesinos would reduce pressure causing them to emigrate to the U.S.
- The high prices now paid by U.S. consumers for vegetables and fruits would be reduced.

Mexico—even before NAFTA—has always been of primary importance to the U.S. and is one of the World Bank's main clients, in terms of volume of lending. With respect to water resources, a critical matter in mostly semi-arid Mexico, the Bank has likewise maintained a strong presence. During the years 1970-75, the Bank and the UNDP assisted Mexico in preparation of a *Plan Nacional Hidraulico* (PNH or National Water Plan). A unit of four staff members, with the author as leader, spent half its time during a 4-year period assisting in preparation of the PNH.[5][6][7] The PNH was a breakthrough and an innovation. As far as is known, no other nation has prepared such an all-embracing plan.

Published in 1975, the PNH was revised and updated in 1980.[8] The World Bank was not involved in the revision which was a pity since the Bank's continuity with the questions concerned was largely lost. This lack of continuity has importance considering that some of the more important recommendations in the original PNH were not carried out.

One in particular, that continues to be of primary importance, concerns better use of land along Mexico's Gulf Coast. This is a zone of relatively ample rainfall (Fig. 6-1) that is devoted to large, low-intensive cattle ranches. Despite a severe shortage of arable land in the country, the ranch owners do not want government-sponsored improvements through drainage and/or irrigation projects, which under Mexican law, limit the size of landholdings to ten hectares.

Mexico, supported by the World Bank, did proceed with a project aiming to speed development in tropical-humid Gulf Coast, which, although covering a relatively small area, has done some good. The program, called "El Programa de Desarrollo Rural Integrado para el Tropico Humedo (PRODERITH)," had substantial World Bank financial support and technical assistance by indigenous agricultural-research agencies, by the Soil Conservation Service of the U.S. and by FAO. It covered 100,000 ha and was supposed to have been followed by a second similar project. An earlier project in the region called "Plan Chontalpa" had been initiated in 1966 with support from the Interamerican Development Bank. The project, which covered 75,000 ha, had mixed success, apparently due to inadequate planning for flood control and drainage. Most of Mexico's petroleum deposits are in the Gulf Coast and the region already possesses considerable infrastructure in the form of roads and major dams (for hyroelectricity and flood control and, to a limited extent for irrigation).

Mexico's achievements in irrigation of its arid and semi-arid regions have been impressive —over 5 million ha under irrigation—and it has a program for improving the yields and efficiency of water use in these regions. There is a pressing need to grow more food for its increasing population and for export of high-value vegetables and fruits, mainly under irrigation.

Under NAFTA, the U.S. market for Mexican vegetables and fruits should be virtually unlimited. Increased trade in these items would bring many benefits: to both the Mexican and the U.S. economies.

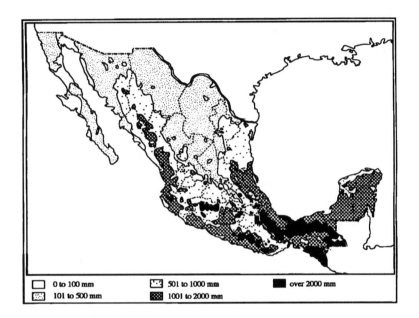

Fig. 6-1. Mexico: Average Annual Rainfall

- Mexico would be better able to buy more U.S. industrial goods, and agricultural commodities too, like corn which in the U.S. is produced in massive industrial-type operations. In Mexico, corn should be replaced by labor-intensive crops like vegetables and fruits.
- The increase in Mexican demand for U.S. products would create jobs in the U.S.
- Increased income for Mexican campesinos would reduce pressure causing them to emigrate to the U.S.
- The high prices now paid by U.S. consumers for vegetables and fruits would be reduced.

The World Bank has continued to lend large sums to Mexico for agriculture, mainly to its banks that relend for short-term credits to farmers, especially *big* farmers. Now that Mexico has just about exhausted all possibilities for further irrigation of its arid and semi-arid regions, it must give more attention to its semi-humid Gulf Coast. The Bank is the agency in the best position to exert pressure for the carrying out of the needed reforms to end the low-intensity use in the Gulf Coast and to restrain the growing inequality of incomes—a leading cause of the current social unrest.

Brazil

Population in 1997: 160,300,000
Population in 2025: 212,900,000
Fertility rate: 3.1
Per capita GNP (US$): 3,640

Population growth rate: 2.5%
Area: 8,544,000 km^2
Life expectancy: 67 years
Percent urban: 76

The Pantanal

With respect to land ownership, Brazil suffers from extreme inequality. A case in point is that of *The Pantanal* in southwestern Brazil (Fig. 6-2) whose extent, as previously mentioned, may be as much as 40,000,000 ha, with about half in Brazil and the rest mainly in Paraguay, with a smaller amount in Bolivia. In the Brazilian part, almost all the land is held by very large cattle ranchers, some holding as much as 50,000 ha. Much of the Pantanal is flooded during the wet season when cattle are moved to high ground. The highly diverse species of wildlife in the Pantanal are apparently adjusted to the seasonal changes caused by the flooding.

Given the present low degree of utilization of the potential of the Pantanal for agriculture, the Brazilian government has for many years been considering what actions to take and, for this purpose has sought assistance from international organizations including OAS and UNESCO. (Under the aegis of the OAS, the author took part in several missions to Brazil in the years 1976 to 1979, two of which dealt with the Pantanal; in 1996, when visiting the Pantanal as a tourist, he found little evidence of significant change in the intervening twenty years.) Large-scale works for control of the extent and duration of flooding could provide substantial benefits but must be planned cautiously owing to possible negative effects on wildlife and biological diversity.

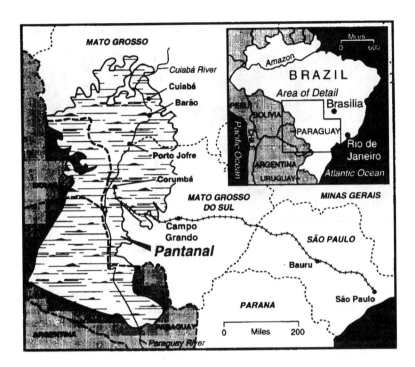

Fig. 6-2. The Pantanal: Brazil, Paraguay and Bolivia

Flood abatement in the Pantanal, owing to reduction in natural valley storage of floods would have the further negative effect of causing increased flooding to lands downstream of the Pantanal.

A large-scale project being considered for the Paraguay River, which traverses the Pantanal from north to south, would enable navigation by ocean-going vessels. How such major works would affect the Pantanal would similarly need cautious consideration.

Northeastern Brazil

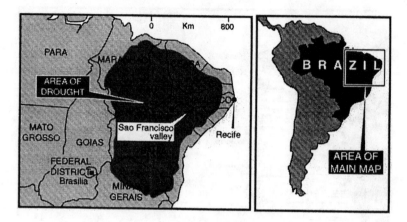

Fig. 6-3. Northeastern Brazil

Brazil has the highest degree of inequity of land and income in the world, which is a basic cause of its social unrest which will surely get worse. In Northeastern Brazil (Fig. 6-3), with a population of 50 million or a third of the entire country, half the inhabitants own no land and are dirt poor.[9]

Besides its dense population and large proportion of landless people, the Northeastern region is vulnerable to both droughts and floods. (The 1992-93 drought was the worst in 40 years.) The droughts cause not only water scarcity but also impairment of water quality, which in turn causes spread of diseases including cholera. Many of the flooding problems appear to be related to poor drainage. Livestock suffer greatly from both droughts and floods.

In the past, families would leave the region at times of drought, many migrating to the industrial cities of the south such as Sao Paulo. But these exits are no longer available and, instead, poor peasants drift to the cities and towns of the region where slums are proliferating. Solutions will require political fortitude in order to deal with the largedisparity in the size of landholdings and the high degree of illiteracy. How best to nurture the Amazon rainforest is a serious matter not only for Brazil but also for the world owing to the diversity of the innumerable species of life that it harbors and its value as a world source of oxygen. Only international action *spearheaded by world leaders* can bring solutions.

World leadership may also be required to assist Brazil in solving its serious problem of landless people in the face of enormous private holdings in many regions, not just in the Pantanal.

The problems of inequitable income, to a considerable extent due to highly inequitable land distribution, may be solved gradually through land reform, which however is being accomplished at exceedingly slow rate.[10] Brazil could profit from the experience of Mexico's land reform which was only partly successful since Mexico paid insufficient attention to the availability of water.

Ecuador

Population in 1997: 12,000,000	Population growth rate: 2.3%
Population in 2025: 18,300,000	Area: 271,700 km^2
Fertility rate: 3.6	Life expectancy: 69 years
Per capita GNP (US$): 1,390	Percent urban: 59

Ecuador presents a case where greed of a few has prevailed over the general welfare. The country has basically two agricultural regions: the *Sierra* and the *Costa*; see Fig. 6-4. The small valleys in the Sierra are fully exploited. The flatlands of the Costa, mainly located in the delta of the Guayas River, are greatly underutilized. Quito, the capital, is in the Sierra. Guayaquil, the country's main port, is in the Costa and has a population of over a million or about 50 percent more than Quito. Both cities, but especially Guayaquil, are growing rapidly owing to in-migration of the rural poor.

In the early 1970s, the Comisión de Estudios para el Desarrollo de la Cuenca de Guayas (CEDEGE) promoted the construction of the Daule-Peripa dam, which it claimed would bring great benefit to the lower Guayas Valley (Fig. 6-5) and to the adjoining but distant Santa Elena peninsula where rainfall is only about 200 mm (compares with about 1500 mm in the Lower Guayas). CEDEGE applied to the World Bank for financing of Daule-Peripa but the Division concerned, of which the author was Chief, after examining the matter carefully, recommended rejection of the application despite active lobbying carried out by CEDEGE's Executive Director.

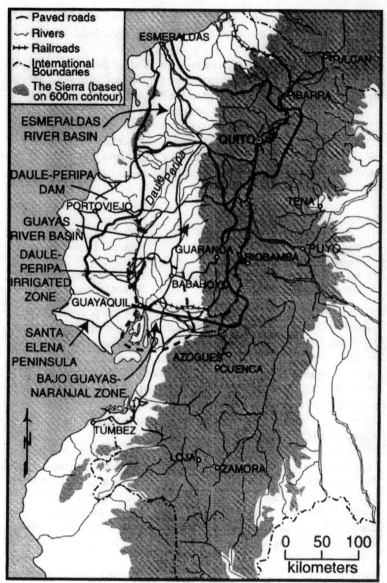

Fig. 6-4. Ecuador's Sierra and Costa

The Division's grounds were that it would be far more beneficial to concentrate on the *drainage and flood control* problems of the Lower Guayas Valley and that, at a later stage, water for *supplemental irrigation* could be obtained from groundwater. The available information showed that the quantity of water available from groundwater would far exceed that from Daule-Peripa and would cost far less per unit. It was also felt that the exorbitant cost of the dam and the aqueducts needed to serve a few large landowners in the Santa Elena peninsula was not only highly uneconomic, it was also very inequitable.

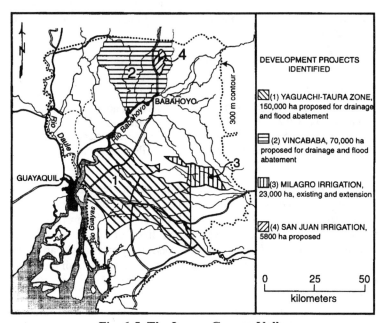

DEVELOPMENT PROJECTS
IDENTIFIED

(1) YAGUACHI-TAURA ZONE, 150,000 ha proposed for drainage and flood abatement

(2) VINCABABA, 70,000 ha proposed for drainage and flood abatement

(3) MILAGRO IRRIGATION, 23,000 ha, existing and extension

(4) SAN JUAN IRRIGATION, 5800 ha proposed

0   25   50
kilometers

Fig. 6-5. The Lower Guayas Valley

The Bank's higher officials, despite pressure from the Executive Director representing Ecuador on the Bank's Board, agreed with the Division, which meant turning down the application for the financing of Daule-Peripa. CEDEGE then made the same application to the Inter-American Development Bank (IADB). Despite information sent to the

U.S. Executive Director on the Board of IADB stating in detail the reasons for turning down the loan for Daule-Peripa, he was out-voted. Daule-Peripa was financed by IADB and it was built.

The problems of poor drainage and flooding persisted and even got worse. Major roads were constructed traversing the region without consideration of drainage needs, thus exacerbating the drainage problems. In 1987, based on a grant from the Netherlands, a consulting firm of that nationality began work on a feasibility study, completed in 1990. The study proposed a first-phase development that would provide flood protection for 184,000 ha and drainage improvements for 60,500 ha. Very important: 3,300 smalholders with 10 ha each would be settled and small-farmers' organizations would be formed plus various environmental and conservation initiatives. Financing would be by the Netherlands and the World Bank.[10]

Peru

Population in 1997: 24,400,000	Population growth rate: 2.2%
Population in 2025: 35,500,000	Area: 1,254,000 km^2
Fertility rate: 3.5	Life expectancy: 67 years
Per capita GNP (US$): 2,310	Percent urban: 70

Peru was much in the news during the recent siege of the Japanese embassy by the *Tupac Amaru* guerrillas, followed by strong measures by the Peruvian president that ended by freeing of the hostages taken by the guerrillas but at the cost of the lives of the guerrillas. The prevailing poor social and economic conditions of a large part of the population have been exploited since the early 1980s by both the *Tupac Amaru* and another guerrilla group, the *Sendero Luminoso*, causing serious political instability.

Peru's *Sierra* has limited agricultural value and what there is already fully exploited Yet the *Sierra* is home to the millions that speak Quechua, the language that dates back to the Incas. These people are poverty stricken as half of them are unemployed or under-employed. They migrate to the cities—Cuzco and Lima—seeking but rarely finding employment.

Coca is grown in a border zone between the *Selva* and the *Sierra*. The *Selva* is part of the Amazon tropical rainforest, which although of practically no agricultural value, is important to the planet for reasons described earlier regarding Brazil.

The *Costa* provides 70 percent of Peru's marketed agriculture, from 700,000 ha of land that is fully irrigated. In 1968 a military junta took over the large prevailing estates and turned them into agricultural cooperatives. These were not successful and severe inflation ensured. A satisfactory story is lacking of why the cooperatives failed. Some said it was poor management, others that they were sabotaged by disgruntled former landowners.

About a third of the land in the *Costa* suffers from salinity and waterlogging due to poor drainage and misuse of water. Correction of these conditions has required a program of rehabilitation—mainly drainage works and the establishment of irrigation-district authorities to carry out effective operation and maintenance. Concurrently, reforms are needed in structural policies to change the role of cooperatives—especially sugar cooperatives—from producer to service cooperatives; elimination of *negative* interest rates that had been providing windfall profits to a privileged few, and replacement of rice cultivation—which consumes too much water—by corn.

The World Bank approved one such rehabilitation project in the late 1970s. Relations between Peru and the Bank deteriorated after that but were later restored.

In 1988 the author was engaged by Kredietanstalt für Wiederaufbau (KfW) of Germany to lead a mission to prepare another rehab project. But after two months of work—mainly studying reports and conferring with KfW in Frankfurt—the mission was cancelled owing to strained relations, this time between Peru and KfW. It seems probable that some large Peruvian landowners did not want interference with their private domains.

Various bilateral and multilateral donors have been pressured from time to time to finance some mammoth projects for trans-Andean water diversions. An example is the long-debated Majes project that would presumably benefit lands adjacent to the city of Arequipa in the southeastern desert of Peru. Such pressure should be resisted as the priority for Peru should be to rehabilitate and secure the proper operation and use of *existing* irrigation projects.

Colombia, the Upper Cauca Valley

Data for Colombia as a whole
Population in 1997: 37,400,000   Population growth rate: 2.1%
Population in 2025: 51,300,000   Area: 1,143,000 km^2
Fertility rate: 3.0   Life expectancy: 70 years
Per capita GNP (US$): 1,910   Percent urban: 70

The verdant Upper Cauca Valley (Fig. 6-6), in southwestern
Colombia, has sometimes been referred to as another *Shangri La.*
Although near the equator, the altitude of 1000 m results in a pleasant
sub-tropical climate. The valley is 200 km long and averages 19 km in
width, with an area of 380,000 ha. Located between two ridges of the
Andes, the valley enjoys deliciously cooling *drainage winds* that blow
every afternoon.

Sustainable development of the water resources of the valley started
in 1954 with the formation of the Corporación Autónoma Regional del
Cauca, also known as the CVC, these being the initials of the Cauca,
Valle and Caldas departamentos (provinces) of Colombia concerned.
CVC's success has resulted in its being viewed by many Latin
American pundits as a model to be emulated elsewhere in Latin
America. It is of interest to review the history of CVC to see what made
it a success and what remains to be done for continued development of
the Upper Cauca Valley.[10]

In the early 1950s, a group of forward-looking landowners thought
that what the valley needed was an *integrated approach* to land and
water development of the valley, similar to what had been
accomplished in the U.S. under the Tennessee Valley Authority.
Believing that an *autonomous corporation* like the TVA would be
needed, the group sought and obtained the advice of David Lilienthal, a
former Director of the TVA.

The Board of Directors of the CVC was composed of public-
spirited men headed by an outstanding Executive Director, Bernardo
Garcés. Most of the Board members had been educated abroad and
almost all were successful businessmen or large landowners. The Board
wanted CVC to be *autonomous* and largely independent of the central
government in Bogotá. For initial financing they decided to impose a
four per mil tax on all property in the Cauca Valley, at least in the main
departamento (province) concerned. There was strong opposition by
powerful *hacienda* (ranch) owners and electric-utility companies felt

threatened and were also opposed. But the Board had the Governor of the departamento on their side and prevailed.

Agriculture was the main economic activity of the valley and continues to be of prime importance. Rainfall, which averages 1200 mm annually and comes in two seasons (there are also two dry seasons each year), is enough for most crops, but not for sugarcane, the principal crop, which requires irrigation. There are several large sugarcane plantations in the valley. Several of these own and operate their own *ingenios* (refineries).

Crops other than sugarcane also stand to benefit from irrigation since one out of four years is relatively dry, and one in seven severely dry. Intensification of agriculture, through improvement of yields and cultivation of high-value crops has made progress with assistance from a large internationally-supported center—the *Centro Internacional de Agricultura Tropical* (CIAT)—which was established in 1950 and is located in the valley near the town of Buga.

Most of the valley bottom in the mid-1960s was used for cattle ranches, a relatively low-value utilization of the land in economic terms and still a major activity. The concentration on cattle has a historical basis. The 16th century Spanish conquistadors, who were accustomed to cattle raising in their homeland, took possession of the valley-bottom lands and largely eliminated crop cultivation as practiced by the native Indians. Aerial photos of the valley show the boundaries of the plots farmed by these Indians.

Industry in the valley is growing rapidly, especially in the vicinity of Cali. Cali, when the author came there in 1955, had a population of about 250,000 and an unreliable electricity supply. Today Cali is a booming city of 1½ million. Its growing industrialization and rapid influx of poor rural people are factors—among others—causing water and air pollution, but these are being tackled by the city with the cooperation of the CVC. Cali is of course famous today as the headquarters of the leading Colombian drug cartel.

Based on Lilienthal's advice, CVC engaged three firms as a consortium to do preliminary and detailed planning, for an initial three-year period, and to train staff of CVC to carry on with further planning and with implementation. Knappen-Tippetts-Abbett-McCarthy of New York (KTAM, but later changed to TAMS—Tippetts-Abbett-McCarthy-Stratton—after Theodore Knappen died) was leader of the three-firm consortium and was designated to handle hydraulic engineering and economics; Gibbs & Hill (G&H) of New York for

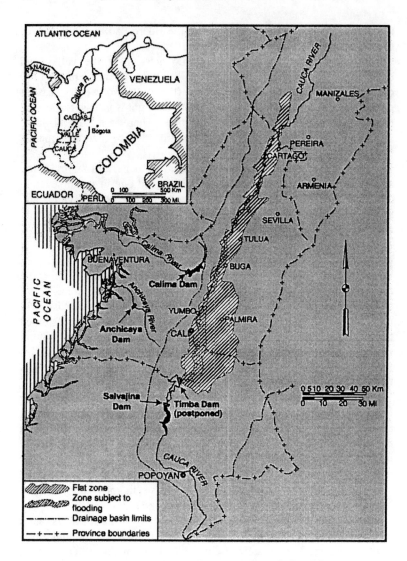

Fig. 6-6. The Upper Cauca Valley, Colombia

design of electric transmission lines and Olarte, Ospina, Arias and Payan (OLAP), a Colombian firm based in Bogotá, to provide general support..

For the consortium, William Voorduin of the New York staff of G&H was designated as "Engineering Director". Voorduin had formerly been with TVA and was known to Lilienthal and had his confidence. Voorduin's reviews of progress were through occasional visits to Cali from New York. All of the analysis and the report writing was done in Cali. The author wore two hats, one as Project Engineer for the consortium, the other as Chief Engineer of the CVC, a position that was turned over to a Colombian when the author left Colombia in 1962. Full-time staff assigned to Cali by the consortium numbered about ten.

The first task was to prepare a *framework plan* in the form of a report entitled "The Unified Development of Power and Water Resources of the Cauca Valley". Completed in January 1956, the report recommended that two projects should go ahead without delay to relieve a pressing electricity shortage: a high-voltage transmission line to serve the entire valley and a hydro plant on the nearby Calima River.

The Calima hydroelectric project would be owned and operated by CVC. But this was opposed by two vested interests: One was CHIDRAL (Central Hidroelectrica del rio Anchicaya) which operated a hydroelectric dam on a river of that name. The other was an agglomeration of coal-mine owners that supplied low-quality coal to a thermal power plant located in the industrial town of Yumbo, near Cali. There were vituperative accounts in the press castigating CVC and their foreign advisers. But Calima was a sound venture and the World Bank indicated its agreement through a loan which the consortium helped negotiate and which included funds for both Calima and the high-voltage transmission line serving the entire valley. Construction of Calima and the transmission line started in 1960 and was completed in 1964.

To deal with Cauca River floods, the report proposed two methods: storage reservoirs at two sites—Timba and Salvajina—that would be *multipurpose,* since water stored to control floods would later be used to augment the dry-season flow of the river; and an embankment to protect a critical urban area at Cali.[11] The large wetland and bird refuge near Buga would be preserved. Salvajina, was built two decades later with financing, in part, from Japanese sources. Timba appears to have been postponed indefinitely.

With respect to water for agriculture and for domestic and industrial use, it would appear that with annual rainfall averaging 1200 mm annually, there would be no problem. However, some years of serious drought had been experienced. Another set of problems related to the rapid growth of the city of Cali, which was stretching the available water supply and causing growing pollution problems.

Some local areas required only flood protection, primarily by means of embankments. Others required irrigation in addition to flood protection. Two such projects that were identified for early construction and are described below were: The Aguablanca Project for flood protection and drainage of a zone adjacent to Cali and the Roldanillo-La Union-Toro (RLT) Project for both flood protection and irrigation.

Land for Urban Growth; Self-Help Housing

The Spanish colonizers, in the first half of the 16th century, located Cali and the other cities and towns in the valley on high ground. But by the 1950s, with no suitable high ground left, a considerable portion of Cali's population had settled in malodorous slums—not unlike the *favelas* of Rio de Janeiro—in the foothills of the Andes.

To remedy this condition, CVC gave high priority to the so-called "Aguablanca Project" for reclamation of 5,000 hectares of low-lying land located southeast of the city and bordering the Cauca River. The reclaimed tract about doubled the usable area of the city.

The project works included 26 km of levee, a 9 km canal to intercept and divert two small streams that used to traverse the area, a drainage pumping station and a pond (with adjoining park) for temporary storage of runoff from storm rainfall.

Concurrently, a scheme for self-help housing was developed making use of the reclaimed land. Building lots about 10 by 30 meters were granted to homeless families and each lot was provided with water and electricity connections and a sewer outlet. The family had to agree to repay the cost of the lot and to build a house using their own labor. A simple machine was supplied for making soil-cement blocks for house walls.

The drainage and flood protection was bound to increase greatly the value of the reclaimed land. A law adopted by the National Government in 1958 required that landowners benefiting should repay CVC for the project cost but apparently the law said noting about

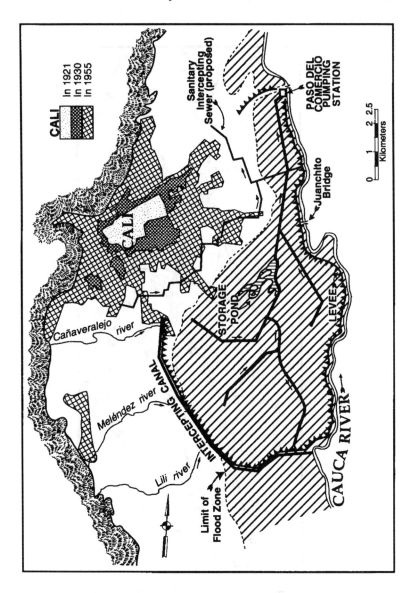

Fig. 6-7. The Aguablanca Project, Cali, Colombia

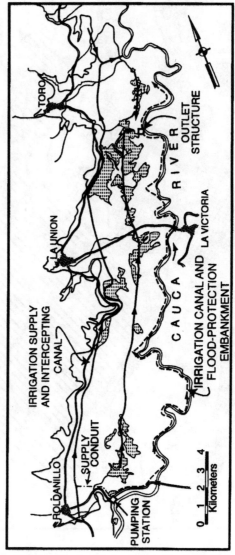

Fig. 6-8. The Roldanillo-La Union-Toro Project, Colombia

payment for the *enhanced* value of the land. I'm not able to say when or how the law was enforced.

Intensifying Agriculture via Irrigation

Despite the annual rainfall of 1200 mm, truly intensive agriculture in the Cauca Valley requires irrigation. (The privately owned sugarcane plantations all have their own irrigation systems.) Following issuance of the Unified Development Report in 1956, CVC planned only one project involving irrigation: the RLT project. It covers an area 11,200 hectares near three small towns: Roldanillo, La Union and Toro (Fig. 6-8). Irrigation water is provided by a pumping station that during the dry season draws water from the Cauca River. Wet-season drainage water is lifted by means of a second pumping station into the Cauca River. One of the feeder canals for irrigation is along the bank of the Cauca River. The excavated material from this canal was used to form an embankment for protection from flooding from the river.

It was hoped that RLT would serve as a *pilot project,* indicating to farmers elsewhere in the valley how irrigation and flood protection could be of benefit to them. A visit to the project in 1974 showed however that the project, although doing well, was not fulfilling its function as a pilot project. It appears that the larger landowners in the valley—most of them *cattlemen*—are not interested. As proposed by some economists, a land tax based on *potential* value of the land may have to be introduced as an incentive for growing high-value crops (or as a *dis*incentive for low-value cattle raising).

It was stated earlier that the Upper Cauca Valley development has been held up as a model for emulation elsewhere in Latin America. From the foregoing description, the following three elements are particularly noteworthy:

- CVC, the lead agency, got off to a good start because of strong leadership by prominent local citizens who were able to achieve autonomy and to put through a tax on local property to finance a significant part of the funds needed.
- Foreign expert advice was sought and obtained but with the understanding that a strong local group of planners and implementers was essential for the planning and execution of further developments in the region.
- Planning has been carried out in a comprehensive manner, taking into account social, economic and environmental factors as well as

purely engineering ones.

Colombia, the Lower Cauca/Magdalena Valleys

Despite its extent, Colombia has limited areas of good to high-quality land for agriculture. The Lower Cauca/Magdalena Valleys, the upper part of which is adjacent to Medellín (Colombia's second largest city with a population of 2.2 million), contain large areas that are either already of good quality or can be raised to that level through artificial means, that is, through drainage and flood control works. In planning such works, it would obviously be essential to consider environmental features with respect to wildlife and pollution.

Some such development, although limited thus far, has already taken place in the lower part of the Magdalena Valley, not far from the Caribbean port cities of Barranquilla, Cartagena and Santa Marta. In the late 1970s, the Government of Colombia expressed an interest in development of the region and obtained some technical assistance from the Netherlands Government for this purpose. On that occasion, the author led a mission of the World Bank to the region and received a favorable impression regarding possibilities for its development. As far as is known, no further action regarding this region has as yet been undertaken.

Haiti

Population in 1997: 6,600,000	Population growth rate: 1.9%
Population in 2025: 9,800,000	Area: 27,700 km^2
Fertility rate: 3.2	Life expectancy: 50 years
Per capita GNP (US$): 250	Percent urban: 32

There is only one river of consequence in the country: the Artibonite. It is Haiti's main source of electricity and its delta is the only compact body of agricultural land in the country. The Peligre Dam on the Artibonite River, completed in 1956, provides the electricity and stores water for irrigation of the Artibonite Plain, which has an area of 38,000 ha (of this 4,500 ha are occupied by villages, roads and canals, leaving 33,500 cultivable).

Deforestation of the watershed of the Artibonite has proceeded unabated owing to the dire need for fuel by the poverty-stricken population. The resulting soil erosion has caused siltation of the Peligre reservoir, which results in lowering of the quantity of water available for irrigation. A World Bank mission by the author in August 1973 showed that infrastructure in the Artibonite Plain had seriously deteriorated. Of its cultivable area of 33,500 ha, 15,400 ha were being irrigated in an "acceptable" manner, 9,600 ha were being irrigated "poorly" and 8,500 ha were being left fallow. By far the principal crop grown was rice: 23,900 ha in the wet season and 22,800 ha in the dry season. But yields, averaging 2 tons per ha, were low.

Studies for renovation of the irrigation and drainage system had been carried out during 1972 with technical assistance provided by the OAS and the French firm SCET. However, the studies were not comprehensive nor in a form suitable for consideration by a financing agency. The mission therefore proposed bringing in a multi-disciplinary team—covering engineering, soils, economics, rural institutions and financial analysis—for a two-year period, with the aim of achieving rapid rehabilitation of the entire Artibonite Plain. As a first step, a new feasibility report would be needed.

he matter was then taken over by FAO in collaboration with the Interamerican Development Bank (IADB). In early 1974 they decided to proceed with the needed feasibility report, but limited to a "pilot area" of 6,000 ha. The mission as well as the Haitian officials concerned felt that this was being over-conservative. It is not known what transpired subsequently .

hat should be of primary concern is the serious soil erosion in the watershed which, because of siltation would greatly reduces the usefulness of the Peligre Dam. While rehabilitation of the downstream infrastructure could be carried out in a relatively short time, solution of the erosion problem will require a reforestation program requiring at least a generation to accomplish. Such a program, which should be started without delay, must include enlistment of the population to prevent future tree-cutting while providing alternate means of su plying cooking fuel.

Dominican Republic

> Population in 1997: 8,200,000   Population growth rate: 2.1%
> Population in 2025: 11,700,000   Area: 48,600 km^2
> Fertility rate: 3.2   Life expectancy: 70 years
> Per capita GNP (US$): 1,460   Percent urban: 61

The Dominican Republic and Haiti share the island of Hispaniola but are quite different. The GNP per capita of the Dominican Republic is almost three times that of Haiti.

On a World Bank mission with an agriculturist, the author was in the Dominican Republic for a month in the Spring of 1964, reconnoitering the country's agricultural potential and identifying possibilities for Bank loans.

The country's *unused* agricultural potential was found to be substantial, provided that proper use could be made of the waters of the two largest rivers of the country—the Yaque del Norte and the Yuna. Sugarcane plantations already existed in the southwestern part (harvesting mainly by Haitians) but exports to the U.S. were stymied by the U.S. protective tariffs for its own plantations, as in Florida and Louisiana. These U.S. tariffs and sugar subsidies are of course highly disadvantageous to both the Latin American countries that grow sugarcane, to U.S. consumer of sugar and to U.S. exporters of industrial goods that these countries would like to buy but don't have the dollars.

Another remarkable economic incongruity was that almost next door to the Dominican Republic was Puerto Rico, which was importing hundreds of millions of dollars worth of fruits and vegetables from the continental U.S. These items could be supplied at far less cost from the Dominican Republic but it would require marketing skills to overcome the technical but mainly administrative bottlenecks in the way.

The ending of the story appears to be favorable as related in an account of the situation in 1988.[12] The World Bank participated in the financing of the physical works for the Yaque del Norte project but continued to be involved through a follow-on loan that concentrated on the social and economic aspects of the development. An element of *good luck* seems to have played a part since the consultant engaged under the follow-up loan, Augustin Merea, a Peruvian, was highly effective in persuading the Dominicans—both the officials and the local farmers—to make changes that led to formation of water users' associations, payment of water charges and improved operation and maintenance. (Merea had been part of the team of foreign experts that assisted the CVC to get started in the Upper Cauca Valley in Colombia in the period when the author was there, 1955-1962.) As the account further states, in addition to the managerial innovations, the Yaque del Norte project took advantage of some technical innovations as well, namely the installation of simple automatic regulating gates on the lateral canals, made possible by the relatively steep slopes of the canals.

Nicaragua

Population in 1997: 4,400,000	Population growth rate: 3.1%
Population in 2025: 7,600,000	Area: 148,600 km^2
Fertility rate: 4.6	Life expectancy: 66 years
Per capita GNP (US$): 380	Percent urban: 63

In 1964 and 1965, the author was sent by the World Bank to review progress on the **Rivas** project. Two issues were found to have been glossed over: first, that most of the benefit would go to a single landowner, none other than President Somoza; second, that an electric-power line to serve the project would be charged entirely to the project even though the power company would garner a benefit for which it would pay nothing.

Numerous *small* landowners that were interviewed said they were against the project because of these unfairnesses. It was concluded that the Bank had made a mistake and the mission recommended cancellation of the ongoing loan for the project. This was accomplished by getting the Nicaraguans themselves *to request* cancellation.

During a second visit to the country, the author had a personal visit with President Somoza. He saw that the Rivas project was dead but wished to interest the Bank in another called **Tuma Viejo**. On an air-reconnaissance flight over the area in the President's private plane with himself as pilot, the author was impressed with the potential of the area which is located east of and not far from Managua, the capital, and he recommended that the Bank follow up and promote investigations while taking into account the land-tenure features so as to avoid the mistake made in the case of the Rivas project.

Notes

1. Proceedings of the Interamerican Dialogue on Water Management, 490 pages, published by the South Florida Water Management District, 3301 Gun Club Road, West Palm Beach, Florida 33406, April 1994.

2. Jeffry S. Wade et al, "Comparative Analysis of the Florida Everglades and the South American Pantanal," Proceedings of the Interamerican Dialogue on Water Management, April 1994, 31-70.

3. Phillip Z. Kirpich, "Priority Regions in Latin America for Water Management," Proceedings of the Interamerican Dialogue on Water Management, April 1994, 247-256.

4. A description of an "Irrigation Management Transfer" program that shows much promise, while revealing further actions needed, is in Research Report 16 of IWMI (formerly IIMI) by Sam H. Johnson III, April 1998. Transfers of responsibility for O&M have been accomplished but collection of water charges and clarification of water rights are problems still to be adquately dealt with.

5. Comisión del Plan Nacional Hidráulico, "Plan Nacional Hidráulico, 1975," Secretaria de Agricultura y Recursos Hidráulicos, Mexico City, 1975.

6. World Bank, "Mexico: National Water Plan, UNDP Project MEX 71/534, Agency Evaluation and Recommendations," November 1976.

7. Gerardo Cruickshank Garcia, "Mexico's National Water Plan," *Water International*, December 1978, 3-8, 17.

8. Comisión del Plan Nacional Hidráulico, "Plan Nacional Hidráulico, 1981", Secretaria de Agricultura y Recursos Hidráulicos, Mexico City, 1981. 7a: Map showing possibilities for expansion of rainfed agriculture, page 40.

9. *The Economist,* "Land Rights, Land Wrongs," July 26, 1997, 30-32.

10. W. Ochs and P. Wittenberg, "The Lower Guayas flood control and drainage project," Proceedings of the Irrigation and Drainage sessions of Water Forum '92, ASCE, 1992, 275-289.

11. Antonio J. Posada and Jeanne de Posada, "The CVC: Challenge to Underdevelopment and Traditionalsim," Colección Aventura del Desarrollo, Bogatá, Colombia, 1966, 226 pages.

12. Phillip Z. Kirpich and Carlos S. Ospina, "Flood Control Aspects of Cauca Valley Development," Journal, Hydraulics Division, ASCE, September 1959, 1-35.

13. Hervé Plusquellec,"The Dominican Republic Takes the Lead,"*The Bank's World,* World Bank, March 1989, 7-8.

Chapter 7

LESSONS FROM PAST CASES, EUROPE

Greece

Population in 1997: 10,500,000	Population growth rate: 0.0%
Population in 2025: 10,200,000	Area: 130,400 km^2
Fertility rate: 1.4	Life expectancy: 77 years
Per capita GNP (US$): 8,210	Percent urban: 72

During the period of civil wars in Greece, from the end of World War II until mid-1950, much financial aid as well as technical assistance flowed from the USA to Greece via the ECA, the Economic Cooperation Administration of the U.S. Government. Two years earlier, with the civil war still raging, ECA had undertaken two basic programs: one for transportation—mainly highways—and the other for electric energy. For the latter, a large U.S. consultant firm, Ebasco Services Inc., had been engaged, with KTAM, another U.S. consultant firm, providing assistance in estimating river flows for possible hydro projects. To do this river-gagging crews had to be sent to the field, which meant traveling to localities which, despite military escort, were still under danger of fire from the Communist rebels.

The transportation and electrification programs of ECA were highly successful. Whereas in 1950 the typical village had neither a paved road nor electricity, by 1965 the reverse was true. Despite the successes of these programs, the ECA mission, and the Greek officials too, had long understood that agriculture was also of high priority. A similar judgement had been reached by FAO in a report dated March 1947.

ECA had had some success in agriculture when, in the early 1950s, it supported a rice-growing scheme in the delta of the Lamia River about 150 km north of Athens. But much more had to be done to make Greece more self-sufficient in food and fiber and to promote exports. Greece, despite almost ideal conditions in many parts of the country for beef and dairy cattle, was importing such products at the rate of $100 million annually, and was ideally situated for exports of fruits and early-season vegetables to northwestern Europe.

Although Greece is two-thirds mountainous and rocky, there are extensive areas of good soils and, while semi-arid or even arid conditions prevail in many parts—like Attica where Athens is located—there are extensive zones of good soils in northern Greece, in the Thessaly Plain, in east-central Greece, in the Agrinion-Messolonghi plains in west-central Greece and in the Pinios plains in the western Peloponnesus. But since these zones have rainfall only during the winter months; irrigation is needed during the summer growing season.

KTAM, with support from ECA, contracted with the Greek Government to prepare "Master Plans" for eight geographical zones aggregating 200,000 ha of potentially irrigable land, varying in size from 2,000 to 70,000 ha. In addition, the contract called for preparation of final construction designs for three diversion dams and desilting works, two to serve the Salonica Plain (60,000 ha) and one for the Agrinion-Messolonghi Plain (70,000 ha), and for repair of flood embankments on the Strymon River in northern Greece.

KTAM accomplished this assignment during the years 1951-54. Initially and for the first two years, the professional staff engaged numbered about 50, of which 10 were Americans and 40 were Greeks. The Greeks, mostly engaged for structural design and for preparation of construction drawings, were eager to gain such employment as that kind of work was still at a standstill owing to the civil war and its aftermath. The 10 Americans on the team were specialists in the various technical fields concerned: hydraulics, soils, geology and subsurface explorations, dams, structures, and specifications. For economic analyses, to the extent needed for preparation of the so-called "Master Plans," a well-qualified Greek was recruited, who later joined the staff of the World Bank.

By 1955 when the author left Greece for Colombia, the work load of the firm's Athens office had increased substantially. Much of this additional work was for clients in nearby countries, notably Turkey and Iraq, and for the U.S. military. For Iraq, the main job was for preparation of a *Report on the Development of the Tigris and Euphrates River System.* Field work was done in Iraq but engineering and economic analyses, and the writing of the report were carried out in the Athens office. For more on Iraq, see Chapter 8.

The work in Turkey was for preparation of construction designs and specifications for a large dam. Taking advantage of the then prevailing calm in the political relations between Turkey and Greece, the firm was able to induce the Turkish authorities to consent to their dam being designed in Athens. At one point, the Turks sent a delegation to Athens to review progress on the designs. From 1953 until early in 1955, the number of staff about doubled owing to the increasing work load.

The KTAM contract required "Master Plans for phased development, through intensive irrigated agriculture, of the eight regions, with analyses to indicate economic justification and financial viability. (As discussed in Chapter 3, the term "master plan" is misleading and inappropriate, and a better term is "framework plan.") It was not yet in fashion and therefore little thought was given at the time to environmental concerns nor to concurrent measures needed, such as agricultural extension to guide farmers in the techniques of irrigation, for the formation of cooperatives for purchase of inputs like fertilizers, seeds and pesticides and machinery, and for marketing arrangements to assure that farmers receive ample prices for their products. In retrospect, the team also lacked an expert on how best to get government agencies to inspire and cooperate with local communities and their leaders.

By mid-1955 construction contracts for the three diversion dams had been let, Orthodox priests had made their benedictions and actual construction had started.

The eight Master Plans, completed about the same time, were clearly of lasting *long-range* benefit to Greece. They set a pattern for future *holistic planning*, whereby economic and social factors are planned concurrently. It should however be noted that little space was given at the time to analysis and recommendations concerning *institution building* and *environmental effects.*.

In 1966, when with the World Bank, the author ran across a report prepared jointly with FAO[12] that was disappointing. The report warned that, for obvious political reasons, irrigation investments were being spread too thinly, that it would be better if fewer projects were undertaken and that these should then be completed expeditiously.

An amendment to the KTAM contract called for preparation of a preliminary study of the so-called Megdova Project, based on diversion of a stream in the Acheloos River basin through a mountain ridge to the Thessaly Plain. Maps and reconnaissance had indicated conditions to be favorable for a high-head hydroelectric peaking station from which the water could be utilized for irrigation of about 15,000 hectares in the plain in the vicinity of the town of Karditsa. General Plastiras, then President of Greece, was from Karditsa and expressed great interest in the project.The preliminary study indicated the project to be highly favorable. A second firm, engaged soon thereafter for preparation of final designs and for contract tendering claimed that KTAM's design, which called for an earthen dam, was faulty and that a concrete thin-arch dam would be better. Since the expertise of the second firm was in thin-concrete rather than earthen dams, the technical reasons given appeared suspect.

Such incidents had occurred in Greece before and on a much bigger scale as, for example, when hydro energy obtainable from the Acheloos River in western Greece was granted at unusually low cost to an aluminum-producing company.

During the early and mid-1980s, while living in Greece, the author learned that several of the master plans were in fact carried out although substantially modified—as well they should have been—which again proves that "master plan" is a faulty term; "framework plan" is a much better term. Visits to some of the areas covered by the master plans showed, from visual inspection, that a large increase in agricultural production had taken place in the intervening years. There were however some negative impressions as well. For example, in one of the areas, where elaborate pressure-piped systems had been installed complete with water meters, the water meters had been vandalized, which meant that farmers were *not* paying water charges and proper maintenance of the system was therefore suffering.

Portugal

Population in 1997: 9,900,000	Population growth rate: 0.0%
Population in 2025: 10,500,000	Area: 89,024 km^2
Fertility rate: 1.4	Life expectancy: 75 years
Per capita GNP (US$): 9,740	Percent urban: 48

The recent history of irrigation in Portugal illustrates once again the importance of holism in planning irrigation developments, also that government investments in irrigation projects are often looked upon as *panaceas,* that may however lead to disappointing results if basic economic and social factors are disregarded.

The first of three visits to Portugal by the author was as part of an 8-person World Bank team that conducted an agricultural sector survey during a six-week period in mid-1969. The pertinent report was issued by the Bank in December 1970 following detailed discussions with the government.[3] The second visit, in May 1983, was as consultant to the Bank for the Tras-os-Montes project in northeast Portugal, and the third, in February 1984, was as consultant to UNESCO for review of the irrigation-sector part of the National Water Plan then under preparation.

Agricultural Sector Survey

The December 1970 report presented a comprehensive review of the agricultural sector along with a series of recommendations that mainly concern macroeconomics or policy questions such as price fixing, subsidies, taxation, farm credit, land tenure and tenancy, and institutional improvements. The report did discuss project ideas for several subsectors including forestry (involved large-scale planting of eucalyptus), livestock (sometimes combined with afforestation), rural roads, rural electrification and fisheries.

With respect to irrigation, the report discussed first the large disparity between the private and state-sponsored scope of irrigation. In 1969, of the total of 620,000 ha irrigated, 590,000 ha were developed by the farmers themselves without significant public assistance. Most of this area was in the northern coastal and piedmont zones of substantial rainfall; see Fig. 7-1. Irrigation was mostly in summer as rainfall during the rest of the year is usually ample. These lands have

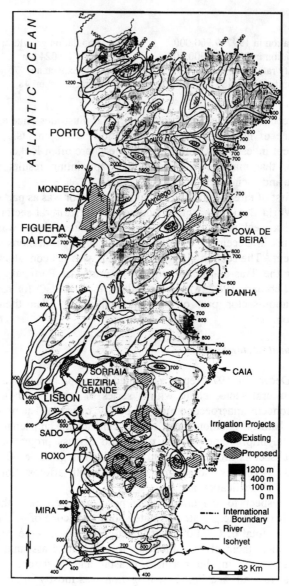

Fig. 7-1. Portugal: Average Annual Rainfall

been irrigated for centuries from springs, perennial rivers and streams, and from shallow wells. The wells were of masonry construction, 3 m in diameter and as much as 10 m deep. Water was lifter by portable centrifugal pumps of 5 to 10 liters per second capacity, driven by one-cylinder diesel or kerosene engines. Each parcel irrigated carried a "water right". The typical holding was small—perhaps 1 ha on the average—and often divided into several non-continuous parts. Much of the land in the North was on terraces, with good land priced at more than 120,000 escudos ($4,200) per ha.

In order to foster expansion of private irrigation, the government was making credit available for small dams, pumps and appurtenances but was having difficulty, owing to the prevailing pattern of very small holdings, to mobilize collateral for loans. Other ideas being considered were:

• Lend to *pump groups* with the loan made to the leader of the group. He would provide water to the members in exchange for plowing or some other service.

• Improve the efficiency of pumping by making electricity available at a reasonable price.

• Reduce the gasoline tax paid by farmers to the nominal amount now paid on kerosene and diesel fuel. This would ;encourage the use of gasoline-driven motors for the pumps which are cheaper and more efficient. Gasoline moreover has other uses on the farm such as for portable sprayers for pesticides.

State-financed irrigation schemes numbering sixteen (Fig. 7-1) were completed in 1969 covering 68,700 ha but only half was actually irrigated. The mission was able to study in some detail six of the larger state-financed schemes totaling 57,500 ha in terms of area commanded but of which 26,500 were actually irrigated. The remaining ten state-financed schemes were not visited; these total 11,200 ha and each is less than 2,500 ha. Each of the six schemes studied was found to face severe difficulties in trying to increase the rate of utilization of the irrigation infrastructure and to raise the output per hectare.

Typically, the projects were in very poor soils and of high cost. The mission judged that, based on experience in other countries, the costs were too high to justify the investments made unless specialty crops of high value and ready marketability could be produced. However, since the projects already existed, the problem was how to put them to best use. One important difficulty concerned the cropping pattern. The two principal crops were rice and tomatoes but neither was rotated so that weeds were proliferating and the level of fertility was dropping. Fruits, sugarbeets, forage crops, cotton and tobacco would merit investigation as rotation or alternate crops, particularly in the sandy soils which require heavy application of water to produce rice. Forage crops would be helpful for improving soil fertility in the sandy soils, both directly and through animal enterprises. A prevailing problem in all state-financed schemes was lack of drainage, correction of which would require further investments. However, to get maximum return, optimal phasing as determined by economic analysis would be needed. The current land tax was both inequitable and too low and therefore did not function as an incentive to get land into its most economic use. Finally, an adjustment in water charges would be essential as well as improvement in the management of the projects. An integral part of all of these problems was the land ownership pattern as some properties were excessively large.

The mission felt that initial efforts with respect to irrigation should be directed toward solution of the drainage, on-farm investment and other problems of the existing irrigation schemes before tackling new project proposals, especially in the semiarid (rainfall 600 mm or less) Alentejo region of the country where possibilities for notable increases in agricultural production through land and water resource development seemed appealing. One such possibility was for a multipurpose project for hydro power as well as for irrigation; it would involve a major dam ("Alqueva Dam") on the Guadiana River in the Alentejo. Negotiations for financing were underway with Kreditanstalt (KfW) of Germany. The mission suggested careful analysis of the economics of the scheme taking into account that as the demand for irrigation increased, the output of primary energy would decrease.

A promising project being considered for early implementation was Leiziria Grande, a 14,000 ha alluvial zone in the delta of the Tejo River near Lisbon. Under development since 1946, some 60 percent of the area was held by a company of 50 shareholders. A problem to be resolved was the project's income distribution impact, considering that part of the project's cost might have to be assumed by the state.

National Water Plan

The author had a second opportunity for an overall look at Portugal's irrigation subsector when in February 1984 he was engaged by UNESCO to review efforts underway for preparation of a National Water Plan. The value of agricultural production in Portugal had dropped seriously during the past two decades; yields, compared with other Mediterranean countries (Spain and Greece), were low; and the country was running an annual agricultural trade deficit of $1 billion. Since consumption of water by agriculture far exceeded its use by other sectors—industrial, domestic or power generation—and since this situation was expected to continue, efforts to prepare a National Water Plan must be based on an analysis of the water requirements of the agricultural sector.

Conclusions of the review were that, as far as the existing state-financed schemes were concerned, water supply was ample, which however does not negate the suggestions of the World Bank review of 1969 with regard to improvement of drainage facilities and correction of managerial and macro-economic factors such as choice of optimum cropping patterns, subsidies, land tenure and collection of water charges.

With respect to new irrigation projects, the review mentions the need, in the case of the extensive semi-arid Algarve region, to carry out planning in a holistic manner. In so doing due weight should be given to the suitability of the region for intensive animal husbandry including cultivation of forage crops based on *supplementary* irrigation, taking into account the available rainfall (averages about 600 mm annually), and for forestry.

Tras-os-Montes Region

Located in the northeast corner of Portugal, this largely mountainous region had in 1983 received the benefit of a loan from the World Bank to further rural development. As a part of the project, three small valleys near the city of Chaves, totaling 9,545 ha, had been identified as having potential for substantial increase in agricultural production if provided with irrigation. With annual rainfall of 500 to 1,000 mm, only supplemental irrigation would have been needed.[4]

A plan involving a storage dam had been promoted but there was doubt on whether this would be the best plan in view of its cost and since it was known that use of groundwater might provide a better solution. The author and a groundwater expert were engaged by the Bank as consultants to assist in studying the matter.

From examination of the available information on groundwater availability, it was concluded that it was reasonably certain that an ample quantity of groundwater could be developed but that this should be confirmed through explorations. The explorations would consist of drilling boreholes, observing the underground strata and carrying out pumping tests.

Explorations of this kind are of course routine when groundwater development is under consideration. The consultants suggested—and the Portuguese officials accepted— that since in their judgement there was a high probability of finding sufficient groundwater, any exploratory well that gave good results should be converted to a production well without delay, thus providing rapid benefits.

Notes

1. World Bank and FAO, "The Development of Agriculture in Greece," December 1966, 121 pages.

2. World Bank, "Agricultural Sector Survey, Portugal" (in two volumes), December 23, 1970.

3. World Bank, Tras-os Montes Rural Development Project, Staff Appraisal Report, May 11, 1982.

Chapter 8

LESSONS FROM PAST CASES, MIDDLE EAST

Perspective

The complex social, political and economic situation of the Middle East—including also its critical water shortages—are deservedly attracting worldwide attention. Symposia, books and articles concerning Middle East water are almost too numerous to list. As gleaned from the references cited,[1] admittedly as influenced by the author's experience in the region,[2] given below is a summary of the current discussions, followed by some conjectures about how the world community might proceed to assist in dealing with the water shortages.

This chapter also contains sections on Egypt, Sudan, Jordan and Iraq. These are countries for which the author, based on personal experience, offers suggestions with regard to future steps to be taken.

The symposia and the written materials are well presented but observers and readers are left perplexed. Although profound understanding of the underlying complexities is displayed and some of the actions that must follow are described, given the political difficulties, how sure can one be that these actions will actually follow?

References are made to various United Nations bodies including UNEP, UNDP, FAO AND UNESCO and also to international financing agencies, especially the World Bank. It is implied that these groups must work in a coordinated way to help solve the Middle East water crisis. Case histories are cited wherein conflicts were averted such as for the Indus River, involving India and Pakistan, and the Colorado River, which involved the United States, Mexico and several US states. In the former case, resolution came through a treaty, which however took a decade of negotiation under the auspices of the World Bank whose president at the time took a personal interest.

Complex and important as it was, the water situation of the Indus was, relatively speaking, less complex and crucial than that of the Middle East. In the latter case, not two but eight important countries are directly involved and all have high rates of population growth: Turkey, Iraq, Syria, Lebanon, Israel, Jordan, Egypt and Sudan. Two adjoining ones—also populous and important—are indirectly involved: Saudi Arabia and Ethiopia. The region is of primary concern to the United States and other western nations owing to its oil riches and the fact that two of these countries—Egypt and Israel—have been, since 1977, major allies and recipients of US aid money.

All discussers of Middle East problems clearly recognize the complexities and massive external assistance that will be needed for studies, negotiations and financing. Two of the discussers, John Kolars, a professor of Near Eastern Studies, and Aaron Wolf, a professor of geography, point to the need for holistic approaches wherein more than water is taken into account. They mention in particular oil!

Water is becoming extremely scarce in the Middle East but, to the extent that it is available, it is renewable. Oil, now plentiful in some of the Middle Eastern countries (Iraq, Iran, Saudi Arabia, Kuwait and the Emirates) is not renewable and—nobody knows for sure—may be gone in 50 years or less. Macro-economic planning, as advocated by Kolars, would presumably deal with mutually beneficial arrangements involving oil-water (or water-oil) trades. Interesting corollary issues would be (a) whether expensive distillation of sea-water for agricultural use, as now practiced by Saudi Arabia, could gradually be eliminated and (b) whether Sudan, with underutilized land and water, could supply low-cost food to the nearby water-short countries.

On the question of massive external support, the discussers cite the UN agencies just mentioned and, more particularly, the World Bank. Biswas decries the current soft approach of the international organizations including the World Bank and says this attitude has to change. It may in fact already be changing. The Bank is now giving much attention to Middle East water issues and has recently issued some reports on the topic.[3] The Bank has also recently decided to be more open in revealing the content of some of its internal documents.

These moves may not, however, silence some critics who believe the Bank should be more activist. For example, the Bank, under its rules, will not finance any water-resource development project affecting more than one country in the absence of firm agreements (treaties) among the countries involved. But it will not actively *promote* such treaties. The India-Pakistan Indus treaty, which was promoted by the Bank, was an exception.

Massive external support would have to cover four main components: technology, institutions and their management, negotiations among the riparian nations and finance. All of these would have to proceed concurrently. Regarding technology, three of the discussers mention at length lack of hydrologic data and—of equal or perhaps greater importance—lack of data on land capability, especially in Syria and Iraq. According to Kolars, Syria's soils in the Euphrates basin are notoriously gypsiferous and saline. Ilter Turan, a Turkish political scientist and professor, similarly points to the lack of adequate data on hydrologic and land capability. It would thus appear that the Turks, when preparing their so-called Master Plan for the Southeastern Anatolia Development Project (Turkish acronym GAP), did not or were not able to give consideration to these factors, at least with respect to the downstream riparians, namely, Syria and Iraq..

With further reference to Iraq, as described later in this chapter, various events, particularly the Iran-Iraq and Gulf wars, have severely interfered with agricultural development.

Reaching long-term or even medium-term solutions for Middle East water, will be arduous, costly and time-consuming. Wolf signals that negotiations, to the extent possible, should be based on two underlying principles: equity and control—equity in the allocation of water, and control of sources by users. He feels that if these contentious issues are faced early on, valuable breathing space can be gained.

In any case, it seems clear that massive external intervention is urgent and with little delay. The UN, backed up by other leading agencies, notably the World Bank, would be the logical body to undertake the task which, clearly monumental, would have to be based on a preliminary examination outlining the strategy and designating priorities. The UN has tackled complex water-resource planning in the past, the leading example being that of the Mekong River basin. That effort was apparently *over-zealous* and not in accord with regional desires. Syed S. Kirmani, a well-known Pakistani water-resource professional and a former World Bank Director, in a 1990 article[1] stated that the UN's objective for developing the Mekong was not shared by the riparian countries, that the role of these countries was only nominal and that they were skeptical as to whether the grand scheme and gigantic projects contemplated would ever be financed and implemented.

Furthermore, as in the case of peacekeeping tasks that the UN has been and still is carrying out, the UN will need strong support from leading countries, especially the United States and the other industrialized countries and such support will not be forthcoming unless the political leaders of these countries commit themselves. The author and other water-resource professionals feel that an urgent task of these professionals is to inform and educate the general public and ultimately the political leaders that resolving the Middle East water crisis is urgent and imperative, not only for the countries directly concerned, but also as a matter of self-interest.

Egypt

Population in 1997: 27,900,000	Population growth rate: 2.1%
Population in 2025: 46,900,000	Area: 2,505,000 km^2
Fertility rate: 5.0	
Life expectancy: 51 years	
Per capita GNP (US$): less than $765	Percent urban: 27

Arid Egypt is faced by a steadily increasing demand for more water, caused by a rapidly growing and urbanizing population. The Nile, almost the only source (Fig. 8-1), has a limited supply, besides which, upstream countries, mainly Ethiopia and Sudan, may want to increase their shares of Nile water. The difficult task that Egypt faces, which involves complex and not fully understood interrelationships, was well described in a 1981 issue of *The Economist.*[4]

The account given herein describes first the fairly massive water-planning effort undertaken in the late 1970s, with which the author gained some familiarity through a review he led on behalf of the World Bank. Subsequent efforts are then described based mainly on articles from publications of the World Bank and the United Nations Development Programme (UNDP), from technical journals such as *Water International*, and from the news media.

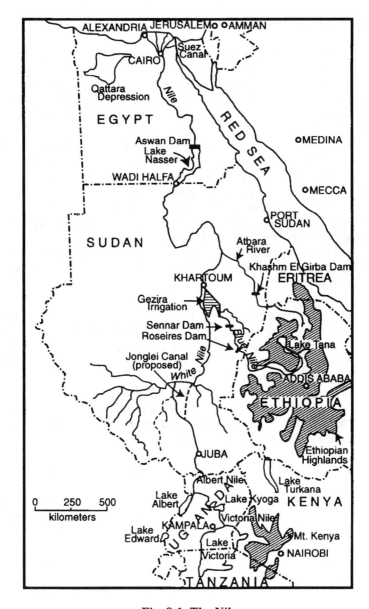

Fig. 8-1. The Nile

The Water Master Plan

A tripartite agreement among the Government of Egypt, represented by the Ministry of Irrigation (MOI); the United Nations Development Programme (UNDP); and the World Bank, as executing agency, was reached in January 1977. It called for preparation of a "Plan for Water Resources Development and Use" also referred to as a "Water Master Plan (WMP)."

Technical Reviews of the WMP were carried out in February 1978, March 1979, September 1979 and November 1979. The author was leader of the team that conducted the last one, which led to conclusions as set forth in two reports, dated May 1, 1981[5] and July 14, 1981.[6] Concurrently, the Bank, which had been making many loans to Egypt for irrigation projects, conducted a "Technical Review of the Irrigation Subsector," described later in this chapter.

The main points of the Technical Review of the WMP of November 1979, as taken from the summary in the May 1, 1981 report, were as follows:

- The High Aswan Dam, completed in 1970, achieved spectacular results in terms of flood control and power generation but not in terms of agricultural output. Since the mid 1960s output growth has been noticeably below the 3.6 percent annual growth rate of the decade preceding the dam.
- The large additions to irrigation water deriving from the dam has had deleterious effects on groundwater levels. This may explain the low rate of agricultural growth and has forced initiation of a country-wide drainage program that has absorbed the major part of the MOI's capital budget.
- The potentialities of the High Dam plus the increased availability of foreign aid make auspicious a new effort to bring new lands into production as in the region east of the Suez Canal. Concurrently, studies of the efficiency of water use at the farm level, being carried out in collaboration with Colorado State University, need to be continued.
- The **Old Lands** (5.8 million feddans or 2.4 million ha), which are lands cultivated before completion of the High Dam, must be the main source of growth in agricultural production. However, the report does not attempt to discuss the changes in policies and incentives that are needed to bring about such increases. The report

concentrates instead on the drainage and irrigation investments, with three major components: (a). Considering that at least half of the Old Lands are constrained by inadequate drainage, the drainage program, which might require another 15 years to accomplish, should have priority. (b) Repair of the irrigation system's structures and equipment, much of which is in or near a state of collapse. (c) Modernization of the irrigation system including (i) increasing canal capacities where needed, (ii) converting canals to gravity flow thus eliminating animal-driven *sakias* and/or motor-driven pumps and (iii) improving on-farm water management to achieve higher crop yields. Also needed are stringent controls to prevent loss of good-quality lands to non-agricultural use, estimated at 0.5 percent annually.

- The potential of the **Old-New Lands** (900,000 feddans or 380,000 ha), which are lands brought into the irrigation network after completion of the High Dam, has not been adequately realized. In areas developed through smallholders, a reasonable level of production has been achieved but not in areas exploited through public-sector companies. Both types have been constrained by rapidly rising water tables.

- **New Lands** that have been identified for development over the next two decades cover 2.2 million feddans or 920,000 ha. Included are 125,000 feddans in the west delta supplied by the Nasr Canal, and 1,290,000 feddans in the east delta of which 585,000 supplied by the Al Salam Canal and 705,000 by the Ismailiya Canal. There are adequate resources studies, mainly relating to soils for the east delta but not for the west delta. It is moreover known that soil conditions in the Al Salam area are highly variable and that the Ismailiya area contains many sandy soils. Development of the New Lands, possibly not justifiable from a strictly economic viewpoint, must proceed in order to provide sources of food and employment and as a means of strengthening national security. The carrying out of resource studies for the El Salaam and Ismailiya areas should receive priority.

- Jonglei I (see discussion below), the first water augmentation project to reduce evaporation losses in the marshes of southern Sudan, is expected to begin operation in 1985 or 1986. Three other projects in the same general area are under consideration for construction before the end of the century. Egypt will begin to need the additional water after 1990. [Neither Jonglei I nor the other projects have proceeded owing inter alia to the political instability in Sudan.]

Two topics that in the author's opinion did not receive adequate treatment in the WMP and therefore in the May and July 1981 reports are the following:

- The summary in Annex 4 of the May 1981 report (a summary has importance since it is usually the only portion that busy executives read; unfortunately, it was not included in the July 1981 report) contains a sentence in paragraph vii: "This report does not attempt to discuss the sort of changes in policies and incentives which are needed to bring about such increases [growth of agricultural production]." Since such changes are badly needed, omission of a discussion of policies and incentives was, in the opinion of the author, a weakness of the report.
- There is no discussion of future major projects that will involve international cooperation, except for a brief mention of the [now indefinitely delayed] Jonglei I project in Southern Sudan.

Subsequent events up to 1991 are described in an article by M.A. Abu-Zeid and M.A. Rady.[7] These men were respectively chairman of Egypt's Water Resources Center and director of Egypt's Water Management Research Institute. Besides policy questions, the article described new administrative and institutional arrangements and environmental issues. Among key observations in the article are the following:

- Since the overall performance of state farms was inefficient, a policy was implemented to allocate up to 60 percent of new lands to economically disadvantaged groups and to private investors with adequate capital to develop their own farms. A recent news item in the New York Times indicated that serious problems relating to land ownership remain to be worked out.[8]
- Farmers pay no irrigation water charges, although they do pay indirectly through land taxes. Before water pricing can be introduced, several obstacles have to be overcome including the Islamic precept that water is a free resource, the fact that the volume of water supplied to individual farmers is not measured and the further fact that farmers are powerful politically. The Ministry of Public Works and Water Resources (MPWWR), with assistance from the U.S. Agency for International Development,

has begun work on water pricing.

- Limitations of the irrigation system include small fragmented landholdings, lack of a continuous water supply, which discourages modern methods such as sprinkler or drip; conveyance losses between canal offtakes and irrigation outlets of 25 percent and between irrigation outlets and fields of 11 percent; and reluctance of farmers to irrigate at night.
- Farmers' organizations are needed to assist in carrying out needed improvements to mitigate these limitations but also to accomplish successful operation and maintenance of the irrigation system.
- Construction of an extensive drainage system to alleviate salinity and waterlogging should continue to receive priority.
- Groundwater contamination from fertilizers and pesticides needs vigilance and control.
- Pilot projects are needed to find best ways to utilize wastewater as a source of irrigation water.
- Nine countries share the Nile. Early cooperation began in 1953 with construction of the Owen Fall Dam in Uganda for which Egypt paid compensation for raising the water level. In 1959, Egypt and Sudan signed the Nile Waters Agreement and established a permanent Joint Technical Commission on the Nile which meets four times a year. In 1964 the commission began to cooperate with countries of the Equatorial Lakes Region which led to the establishment of a comprehensive regional hydrological network. In the late 1970s Egypt and Sudan proposed a comprehensive mechanism to provide continuous cooperation among all riparians but this objective has not been achieved.

An analysis prepared in 1996 with financial support of the Canadian International Development Agency indicated a "very critical situation regarding the match between available water and requirements."[9]

A 1992 discussion of the competition for Nile water by the nine riparians states that the period of water abundance is at an end and that it is imperative to take a basin-wide perspective on future water planning for the Nile. Regarding major projects to increase the usable flow of the Nile, it is pointed out that, while the Jonglei Canal Project (see below) has been the focus of intense media attention over the last two decades, from a water-control perspective a series of dams on the Blue Nile in Ethiopia would be far greater importance for Egypt, Sudan and Ethiopia. A major study of the Blue Nile in Ethiopia was carried out from 1958 to 1963 by the United States Bureau of Reclamation but has received little attention since that time.[10]

In 1994, with financial support of the Canadian International Development Agency, a conference of Nile Basin countries was held in Khartoum. All parties agreed on the need for continued cooperation and that an appropriate international body should be selected as a regional focal point.[11]

The Jonglei Project for drainage of the vast Sudd marshes in southern Sudan would provide important benefits to both Sudan and Egypt.[12] Marked reduction of evaporation from the marshes would materially augment the flow of the White Nile. However, the protracted hostilities between the peoples of North and South Sudan do not allow the project to proceed.

A 1994 published discussion on the Nile Basin, mainly from the point of view of Sudan, described technical assistance being provided by various agencies of the UN: Hydromet Project of the Equatorial Lakes [hydrologic measurements in the upper basin of the White Nile] by UNDP, diagnostic study of environmentally sound management of the basin water resources by UNEP, and support for a hydraulic research station in Sudan, by UNESCO.[13] The discussion also emphasized that severe soil erosion in the Ethiopian Highlands, caused by destruction of forests, would have serious consequences, among which would be loss of storage in the Roseires reservoir. With the numerous studies and efforts underway, an obvious question is whether they are being adequately coordinated.

An article in a 1997 issue of *The Economist* described two ongoing strenuous efforts to get more land under cultivation. One of these, a scheme for irrigating New Lands in the Sinai Peninsula served by the previously mentioned Al Salam Canal, should be ready soon. The other, more ambitious but problematical, is the New Delta project which would take water from Lake Nasser behind the High Dam at Aswan and send it for 500 km to link a string of remote desert oases.[14]

The Irrigation Subsector

Concurrent with the Technical Review of the Water Master Plan, another mission of the World Bank was in Egypt carrying out an Irrigation Subsector Review. The summary in the draft report of the mission dated March 28, 1981,[15] substantially corroborates what was stated in the WMP report. In addition it contains descriptions of future projects that may be suitable for external financing in the short term (succeeding five years) and recommends that the two Project Preparation Units, one in the Ministry of Irrigation and the other in the Ministry of Land Reclamation, undertake to prepare the relevant feasibility studies. The report proposes a World Bank credit (low-interest loan) by the Bank of $6.9 million to pay for foreign consultants to assist the PPUs.

As in the case of the Bank's review of the WMP, the March 1981 draft report on the irrigation subsector, in paragraph vii of the summary, contains a statement: "This report does not attempt to discuss the sort of changes in policies and incentives which are needed to bring about such increases [in growth of agricultural production]." However, this is not consistent with statements elsewhere in the report, as in the section entitled "Irrigation Water Management in Annex 4:

> The Water Research Center of the Ministry of Irrigation is presently carrying out a study of irrigation water management practices in collaboration with Colorado State University. In the course of the study, the various combinations of policy and infrastructural options which could lead to improved irrigation water management practices will be considered.

Another example of this inconsistency results from the discussion in Annex 6 (entitled Livestock and Irrigation Modernization) of the almost universal practice of using animal-driven *sakias* s to pump water from the *mesqas* (delivery channels linking MOI's distribution canals and farmers' fields. Although mechanized pumps are gradually replacing the sakias, thus far only 20 percent of the animals originally used have been replaced. The report brings out that pricing policies that keep basic food crop prices at low levels discourage farmers from shifting away from the large area of the winter-forage Egyptian clover (berseem) to food crops.

Irrigation Improvement Project (IIP)

The IIP consists of a series of pilot projects on Old Lands, totaling 400,000 feddans (170,000 ha) jointly funded by the Government of Egypt and USAID. The objectives have been to modernize command-area-canal and mesqa delivery systems, organize mesqa water users into Water User Associations (WUAs) and create an Irrigation Advisory Service to provide technical assistance.[16] The aim is to complete the organization of 1200 WUAs, improve their mesqas and modernize all of the canals serving these WUAs. The area served by a single mesqa is from 50 to 500 feddans but the author guesses that the average is about 100 feddans or about 50 ha involving 25 farmers whose holding is about 2 ha on the average. The area modernized would thus be about 60,000 ha, or only 2.5% of the area of the Old Lands. Still, if the project continues to be successful, it could pick up speed as farmers adjacent to the pilot projects become convinced of the potential benefits.

With respect to the introduction of water charges, in 1995 the International Irrigation Management Institute (IIMI) was asked by USAID to conduct studies to assist the Government in formulating a rational approach to sharing costs of water services, especially for irrigation.[17] It was concluded that charges for water services would not induce significant changes in cropping patterns or improvements in system performance because the cost of system operation is low in relation to the benefits of irrigation. Further, until revised accounting procedures are in place, charges cannot be linked to service at the local level, although there would be reduction of the financial burden on government. IIMI's report ends by pointing out that, although under the current system, which operates as a demand system with enough water to meet the vast majority of needs, this situation could change if water is drawn off for irrigating the New Lands or as a result of lower water quality caused by pollution. If that happens, clarification of water rights and of water service would be required. In the author's opinion, the questions involved require continuous close scrutiny including possible systems of rationing, either as a substitute or supplement for water charges.

The officials in charge of irrigation in Egypt are right in not being complacent about their water problems and are taking steps to conserve this vital resource. Given Egypt's importance in the Middle East and in the World, the international agencies, with support from leading governments, should take steps to resolve how the waters of the Nile can be better managed on behalf of the nine riparian states concerned. Chapter 9 discusses this question further.

Sudan

Population in 1997: 27,900,000	Population growth rate: 2.1%
Population in 2025: 46,900,000	Area: 2,505,000 km^2
Fertility rate: 5.0	
Life expectancy: 51 years	
Per capita GNP (US$): less than $765	Percent urban: 27

The northern two thirds of Sudan, settled by Arab-African groups, is largely desert with rainfall of 100 mm or less in the extreme north increasing to 160 mm at Khartoum and 470 mm at the southern extremity of the Gezira project area; water from the Nile is therefore essential. In the southern third, settled by Nilotic groups, rainfall reaches 1,000 mm.

Although over a third of Sudan is arable, only 5 percent is under cultivation with over half of the people engaged in subsistence farming. Cotton, grown mainly in the Gezira region between the Blue and White Niles, is the biggest cash crop, providing 43 percent of export revenues.

Long considered the potential breadbasket of Africa, Sudan's development has been hindered by inefficient management, deteriorating equipment and an inadequate transportation system. The decades of civil strife between the North and the South has been a further major cause.

From 1979 to 1988, the author carried out six missions to Sudan as consultant to the World Bank. The missions dealt with two large irrigation projects, Gezira with 850,000 ha and Rahad with 250,000 ha, which account for 42 percent of the national total of 2,600,000 ha, and reviews of priorities in the irrigation sector. These reviews led to formulation of a project called "National Irrigation Rehabilitation Project (NIRP)."

Foreign financial aid, bilateral as well as multilateral, had flowed to Sudan at the rate of $800 million a year but was largely discontinued following the military coup of 1989. Besides financial aid, the country had benefited from technical assistance provided by leading international organizations. Yet Sudan, despite its huge potential, has enjoyed only limited progress. Its population continues to suffer from widespread poverty, which is a leading cause of its political instability.

Status of National Water Planning

A so-called "Master Plan" for the Nile was prepared in 1982. Two variations followed in 1984 and 1985. Preparation was by leading British, French and Swedish consulting firms, and the U.S. Bureau of Reclamation. Financial support was provided by USAID and UNDP.

The Master Plan was prepared with only minimal participation by Sudanese planners (engineers, agriculturists, economists and sociologists). No permanent Sudanese interdisciplinary core group was formed able to refine and update the plan. As a result, Sudan suffers weaknesses in its capacity to carry out effective water-resource planning, owing to:

- Lack of ability to evaluate departures from assumptions and scenarios made in previous plans, such as the drought of 1984-85, fuel and energy shortages, new sources of donor financing and oilfield discoveries that could lead to a significantly different development of the White Nile region.
- Lack of a mechanism for dealing with water conflicts within Sudan.
- Lack of an effective agency to monitor and evaluate feasibility studies for specific projects in the water sector.
- The vulnerable position of Sudan in dealing with other countries on international water issues.

The approximately 30 irrigation perimeters in the country may be placed in the following five groups according to hydrologic region (areas in thousands of hectares):

	Existing	Future
White Nile upstream of Malakal	17	122
White Nile, Khartoum to Malakal	210	380
Blue Nile	1,132	1,526
Atbara River	168	408
Main Nile downstream of Khartoum	131	245
	1,658	2,681

The Sudan-Egypt Nile Waters Agreement of 1959 allocated the average flow of the Nile at Aswan of 84 billion m^3 as follows: Sudan 18.5, Egypt 55.5 and loss through evaporation from Aswan reservoir 10. According to the Master Plan, water availability would be more than ample for all perimeters except those of the Blue Nile and Atbara. In the case of the Blue Nile, it was concluded that raising the crest level of the Roseires Dam from 481 m (existing) to 490 m would provide sufficient storage to assure adequate supply for the Blue Nile perimeters while allowing space for 20 years of silt accumulation. A similar conclusion was reached with respect to the Atbara perimeters for which storage would be provided by two dams of which one already existed.

A major hydroelectric development on the main Nile at Merowe in the vicinity of the Fourth Cataract of the Nile, which is about 350 km north of Khartoum, has been under study by the Swedish firm SWECO. The potential was said to exceed 1,000 megawatts. If of that magnitude, cooperation with Egypt on its realization would seem necessary. It is not known whether further studies have been carried out.

As a next stage, a list of needed feasibility studies for near-future projects was agreed upon; in addition, steps were spelled out for corollary efforts including formation of a Water Planning Unit, manpower studies and farm-level pilot schemes.[18] But then little happened until end-1988 when terms of reference were prepared for a foreign consulting firm, engaged for major support in the carrying out of the National Irrigation Rehabilitation Project (NIRP) described below.

How best to set up a permanent arrangement for review and periodic modification of the Master Plan, is a serious matter that continues to be unresolved.

National Irrigation Rehabilitation Project (NIRP)

In October 1988, following severely damaging floods in Sudan, the World Bank sent a large mission there to participate in preparation of an emergency relief program. The author was part of the mission with the additional task of reviewing the status of preparation of the NIRP. He was told that the consulting firm Sir M. MacDonald & Partners, UK, had been chosen to provide major support for carrying out of the NIRP. As a result of the author's review, the following major additions were made to the Terms of Reference of the consulting firm:[19]

- Review of the ongoing Gezira Rehabilitation Project (GRP), described below.
- Minor Canals: Redesign, and Operation and Maintenance. Of the annual silt deposition in the canal system, amounting to 17 million m^3, three-fourths were in the Minor Canals. Alternatives needing study and testing included: excavation by dragline, as currently practiced; excavation and weed cutting by hydraulic excavators; hand methods for weed cutting; herbicides and biological methods.

Further discussion of this topic is given below under the GRP.

- A Review Panel, proposed for the Rosaries Dam Heightening, should liaise closely with the team preparing the NIRP. An alternative worth considering is to pump surplus White Nile water to portions of the Gezira scheme. If favorable, heightening of Roseires could be postponed.
- Updating of water balances for the Nile River basin to the extent feasible. Much will depend on concurrent studies and negotiations with Egypt as discussed earlier in this chapter.

A former planning and finance minister has pointed to major policy changes that will be needed in matters such as water-charge systems, food self sufficiency vs. food imports and inter-agency coordination.[20] Some of these changes will hopefully be dealt with under the GRP.

Gezira Rehabilitation Project (GRP)

The Gezira scheme, 900,000 ha in extent, is the world's largest irrigation scheme under a single management and covers almost half of Sudan's irrigated area. Started in the 1920s by a British syndicate, primarily for cultivation of cotton for export, the scheme covered 600,000 ha by 1950. The remaining 300,000 ha were developed in the 1950s and 1960s.

Long-staple cotton, Sudan's principal export and main source of foreign exchange, had a volume of 168,000 tons in 1972-74. The volume dropped to 81,000 tons in 1979-81, causing economic and political difficulties.

The Gezira Rehabilitation Project (GRP), estimated to cost $285 million, is a major undertaking that started in 1985. As spelled out in a 1983 World Bank staff appraisal report,[21] GRP has the following objectives:

- Overcoming the backlog of deferred maintenance of the existing infrastructure, mainly clearing heavy siltation of the irrigation canals.
- Repair of deteriorated canal-control structures.
- New infrastructure including a drainage cum road system, telecommunications and rural water supply.
- "Invisibles" consisting of computerization (inventories, personnel records and tenants' billings) and improved management in a broad sense.

- Preparation of the next-stage intensification project.
- Two Pilot Zones of about 1,100 ha each for carrying out "action research" on actual farmers' plots and on the irrigation canals serving the Pilot Zones.

Success of the "invisibles" portion of GRP would have much significance for Sudan's future. However, strong, innovative leadership would required, which is complicated by the fact that four principal agencies are involved: Sudan Gezira Board (SGB), Ministry of Irrigation (MOI), Agricultural Research Corporation (ARC) and the Rehabilitation Project Management Unit (RPMU).

Another institutional complication results from the lack of clear division of responsibility for water distribution and management, as between SGB and MOI. O&M of the larger canals in the 900,000 ha scheme, called "Mains," "Branches" and "Majors," with a total length of over 2,000 km, is the responsibility of MOI. At the lower end of the scale are the "Abu XX" canals (tertiaries), length about 40,000 km and capacity 125 to 250 L/s, and the "Abu VI" canals (quarternaries) of which there are about 100,000 km with a capacity of 50 L/s; the farmers are responsible for their O&M under the supervision of the SGB.

Between the canals managed by the MOI and the SGB are the "Minors"with a length of about 8,100 km where responsibility may be clear de jure but not de facto. Each Abu XX receives water from a Minor through a Field Outlet Pipe (FOP) of which there are 29,000 in the Gezira scheme. The flow through each FOP used to be controlled by means of a metal gate, which was, however, of faulty design and fell into disuse. (All 29,000 gates are to be replaced under the GRP.)

Water *ghaffirs* employed by SGB used to close the FOP gates at night so as to permit only daytime irrigation. However, disuse, deterioration and theft of the gates (they make desirable cooking utensils) coupled with poor water distribution (both off- and on-farm) has caused wide-spread practice of night irrigation.

Opinion is strongly divided in Sudan on the issue of night irrigation. Those opposed say farmers cannot irrigate efficiently at night, will waste water and not tend their crops adequately. Those in favor say that with continuous 24-hr irrigation, the flow handled by the farmers is much less and that, given the flat terrain and the small basins (about 14 x 14 m) that are employed, presence of the farmer is not needed at night. A further serious disadvantage of daytime-only irrigation is that it requires use of the Minors as night-storage tanks, causing them to be about 10 m wide at full supply level which is much wider than needed for conveyance. The excessive width results in low velocities of flow and heavy siltation of the Minors.

The action research in the Pilot Zones should inter alia help resolve the night storage issue. Among the issues to be researched and tested on actual farmers' plots are: (1) Improved watering and cultivation techniques based on continued use of small basins: (2) watering and cultivation techniques using long furrows and level basins but requiring precision land leveling carried out by laser-guided machinery; (3) optimum watering rates with the above techniques covering also the advantages and disadvantages of night watering; (4) drainage requirements; (5) maintenance of the Abu XXs and Abu VIs, division of labor among the farmers, and use of machinery; (6) labor requirements, economic and financial returns; and (7) health aspects with particular reference to malaria and schistosomiasis (both prevalent in the region).[22]

The long-furrow system (combined with precise leveling and use of siphons) versus continued use of the small-basin system is another subject of contention. It does however seem clear that large-scale adoption of the long-furrow system is bound to be delayed indefinitely if not permanently, given the physical, cost and managerial difficulties involved. the latter difficulty is compounded by the prevailing pattern of small landholdings, generally 4 has but often only 2 ha.

The foregoing sketch again illustrates that innovative management is the key and that appropriate technology (almost none of it high tech) is already available but must be judiciously applied.

From the October 1988 review of the status of preparation of the NIRP, conducted by the author on behalf of the World Bank[23] and from a 1990 World Bank technical paper (which concentrated on technical design matters rather than on institutional and managerial aspects),[24] it was evident that progress on the GRP has been seriously delayed.

Jordan

Population in 1997: 4,400,000	Population growth rate: 3.3%
Population in 2025: 8,500,000	Area: 98,000 km^2
Fertility rate: 5.6	Life expectancy: 66 years
Per capita GNP (US$): I$1,510	Percent urban: 78

Jordan is critically short of water. In 1979, Bernard Chadenet, a Vice President of the World Bank, and the author comprised a mission to assist the government in establishing a National Water Planning System.

Upon arrival, the mission found that the domestic water supply in Amman, the capital city, had just been reduced from twice a week to once a week. Supply available at the time for the Amman-Zerqa urban area amounted to only 25 litres per capita per day (lpcd) compared with a demand that was at least double, which was still low compared with what was enjoyed by cities in the same climatic region: Damascus with 159 lpcd and Aleppo with 90.

The main technical question under consideration at the time was how to increase supply to Amman. Two alternatives for aqueducts to accomplish this had been studied by foreign consultants: one would be 95 km long from the proposed Maqarin Dam on the Yarmouk River to Amman; the other would be only 26 km long, picking up Maqarin water from the East Ghor Main Canal (which draws water from the Yarmouk River and distributes the water for irrigation of the east side of the Jordan Valley) and thence to Amman. Since Amman is 1,000 m above sea level, either alternative would have involved major pumping, especially the latter alternative, since the level of the East Ghor Canal is 100 to 200 m below sea level.

The proposed Maqarin Dam (also known as the "Unity Dam" or the "Al-Wahdeh Dam," the former possibly because the right abutment of the dam would be in Syria and the left abutment in Jordan) would be on the Yarmouk River, a tributary of the Jordan River with practically all of its watershed in Syria. Studies and subsurface explorations for the dam had been underway for some years and, concurrently, negotiations between Jordan and Syria had been proceeding. Syria's agreement is required not only because one of the dam's abutments is in that country but also because Syria has tentative plans for irrigating lands in the watershed of the Yarmouk that could materially reduce the usable flow of the river.

Since the mission was informed that negotiations with Syria were expected to end favorably the mission gave emphasis to consideration of steps needed to proceed with tendering for the Maqarin Dam. With respect to the National Water Planning System, the mission suggested to the Bank that a follow-up mission be sent to draw up terms of reference for 3 or 4 full-time Jordanian technicians to lead the work of a proposed Central Water Board and to prepare an application to the

UNDP for financial assistance in providing 3 or 4 foreign experts. The suggested follow-up mission visited Jordan in 1980.[25]

The negotiations concerning the Maqarin Dam did not however proceed. One writer asserts that this was due to Israeli pressure on the World Bank to withhold its financing of the project.[26] Not having the Maqarin Dam, Jordan has had to look for other, far less promising alternatives that have been described by various writers[27] which include:

- use of brackish water for irrigation
- use of more efficient irrigation techniques, especially drip irrigation for vegetables and fruit orchards
- desert dams and water harvesting
- desalination of brackish water blended with treated wastewater
- groundwater recharge.

For all of these alternatives, Jordan can make use of—and in fact is already making use of—the extensive and sophisticated experience of its neighbor—Israel. Three informative articles by Israeli experts in a World Bank publication[28] caution however that, before transferring advanced technology, careful consideration must be given to several key factors, among them: water quality, particularly mineral and sediment content; efficiency of operation and maintenance of the irrigation and drainage system; effectiveness of agricultural credit and extension; marketing arrangements and others.

In the author's judgement, the foregoing measures may mitigate Jordan's water shortage for a limited time, perhaps a decade or two. It is therefore urgent that Jordan, with help from the international community, resume negotiations with Syria over the Yarmouk. Beyond that, perhaps there is a chance that ultimately the surplus water that Turkey says it has at the mouth of the Seyhan River in its southeast corner can be made available through its so-called "Peace Pipeline," which could supply water to Saudi Arabia and Israel as well. Such a "dream project" must however await settlement of several ongoing political stalemates.

Iraq

Population in 1997: 21,200,000	Population growth rate: 2.8%
Population in 2025: 41,600,000	Area: 402,000 km^2
Fertility rate: 5.7	Life expectancy: 59 years
Per capita GNP (US$): na	Percent urban: 70

A comprehensive planning report, prepared in 1952 on behalf of the Iraqi Development Board and under the editorship of the author, was a first attempt in modern times to evaluate the vast agricultural potential of Iraq.[29] Based on semi-detailed field studies, the estimated area of good arable land, according to the report, was 5.5 million ha of which 3.25 million were irrigated on a partial basis. It was the intention of the Development Board to settle a large proportion, from among the bulk of the population that then owned no land, on the remaining unirrigated 2.25 million ha. The land classification studies had indicated that 6 percent of this land was Class 1 (choice) and 68 percent Class 2 (good, but including heavy clay or gravelly areas, and having medium salinity). A key recommendation of the report was that agricultural practices needed much improvement to increase prevailing low crop yields.

The history of water planning for the Tigris/Euphrates system presented by John Kolars, Professor Emeritus, Department of Near Eastern Studies, University of Michigan, includes a description of events after the mid-1950s.[30] The Development Board's planning was disrupted by the 1958 revolution. From 1970 to 1984 a comprehensive Master Plan was developed with the help of the Soviet Union but it was not available to Kolars. In 1979 Saddam Hussein abolished the Ministry of Agrarian Reform; he also merged the Ministries of Agriculture and Irrigation while reducing the staff by 30 percent. The Iran-Iraq and Gulf Wars diverted attention from agriculture and hydraulic development.

From another source, there was progress in the carrying out of agrarian reform in the years 1958-1977.[31] However, in terms of agricultural production, the expected benefits of the reform failed to materialize, especially with respect to the two main crops, wheat and barley. Poor administration, neglect of cooperatives and failure to control salinity combined to produce erratic crop yields and spread discouragement among the peasant population. A result was large-scale migration by the peasants to the urban areas. To compensate for the loss of rural manpower, foreign—mainly Egyptian—agricultural labor was imported, variously estimated at the time from ¾ to 1½ million.

Turkey's GAP development scheme in the upper Tigris/Euphrates has caused a complex situation that directly affects the downstream riparians—Syria and Iraq—as mentioned in the opening section of this chapter.

Notes

1. References on Middle East Water Conflicts

December 1990 Special Issue on Water, Peace & Conflict Management, *Water International* vol. 15, No. 1. M. Yunus Khan "Boundary Water Conflict Between India and Pakistan" 195-199; Syed . S. Kirmani "Water, Peace and Conflict Management: The Experience of the Indus and Mekong River Basins" 200-205.

January 20, 1991 Thomas L. Friedman, *NY Times* "What the United States Has Taken On In the Gulf, Besides a War."

March 1993 Special Issue on Water in the Middle East, *Water International* vol. 18 No. 1. Ulrich Kuffner, World Bank "Water Transfer and Distribution Schemes," 30-34. David B. Brooks, Intl. Development Research Centre, Ottawa, Canada, "Adjusting the Flow: Two Comments on the Middle East Water Crisis" 35-39. Frederick W. Frey, Dept. of Political Science, Univ. of Pennsylvania "The Political Context of Conflict and Cooperation Over International River Basins" 54-68. Ilter Turan, Faculty of Political Science, Istanbul University "Turkey and the Middle East: Problems and Solutions" 23-29.

1994 "International Waters of the Middle East—From Euphrates-Tigris to Nile" Asit K. Biswas, ed., Oxford University Press. 221 pages. Aaron T. Wolf, Asst. Prof. of Geography, Univ. of Alabama " "A Hydropolitical History of the Nile, Jordan and Euphrates River Basins," 5-43. John Kolars, Prof. Emeritus, Dept. of Near Eastern Studies, University of Michigan " "Problems of International River Management—The Case of the Euphrates" 44-94. Yahia Abdel Mageed, Associated Consultants, Khartoum "The Nile Basin: Lessons from the Past" 156-184.

1996 Ilter Turan, Koç University, Istanbul "Water Problems: Can the United Nations Help? A Discussion with Special Reference to the Middle East" *Water International* 21 1-11.

2. 1994 Phillip Z. Kirpich. Review of book "International Waters of the Middle East—From Euphrates-Tigris to Nile" Asit K. Biswas, ed., in *Intl. Journal of Water Resources Development*, vol. 10 no. 3, 364-367.

3. World Bank, December 31, 1992,"A Strategy for Managing Water in the Middle East and North Africa" Draft of Report No. 11409-ECA/MENA, text 47 pages, summary 6 pages, 6 tables, annex 10 pages, map. July 1994, "A Strategy for Managing Water in the Middle East and North Africa" text 63 pages, summary 9 pages, 6 tables, map. 1996, "From Scarcity to Security—Averting a Water Crisis in the Middle East and North Africa" (expands on the July 1994 World Bank Report "A Strategy for Managing Water in the Middle East and North Africa") 27 pages.

4. March 28, 1981; *The Economist*, "Egypt and Sudan: A raging thirst that not even the Nile can slake," 85-87.

5. May 1,1981; World Bank, draft report "Plan for Water Resource Development and Use, UNDP Project EGY/73/024, Evaluation of Phase One," 21 pages plus four annexes. Annex 4 comprises a 7-page summary.

6. July 14, 1981; UNDP/WB, report, "Agency Evaluation and Recommendations," 21 pages plus three annexes which are the same as the first three annexes of the foregoing.

7. June 1992; "Water Resources Management and Policies in Egypt" M.A. Abu-Zeid and M.A, Rady in "Country Experiences with Water Resources Management; Economic, Institutional, Technological and Environmental Issues," World Bank Technical Paper No. 175, 93-102.

8. Dec. 27, 1997, *NY Times*, "Egypt's Farmers Resist End of Freeze on Rents—New Law Will Leave Many Without Land."

9. 1996 "Comparative Analysis of Egyptian Water Policies" Hussam Fahmy, Nile Water Strategy Research Unit, Qalubia, Egypt; *Water International*, 21, 35-45.

10. 1992 "Opportunities for Regional and International Cooperation in the Nile Basin" Dale Whittington and Elizabeth McClelland, *Water International*, 17, 144-154.

11. 1992 "The Nile 2002: The Vision Toward Cooperation in the Nile Basin" Aly M. Shady, Canadian Intl. Devt. Agency; Ahmad M. Adam and Kamal Ali Mohamed, Min. of Irrig & Water Resources, Sudan; 19, 77-81.

12. 1988 "The Jonglei Canal: Illusion or Reality" Robert O. Collins, Department of History, Univ. of California, *Water International, 13, 144-153.*

13. 1994 "The Nile Basin: Lessons from the Past" Yahia Abdel Mageed [Associated Consultants, Khartoum] in "Waters of the Middle East" edited by Asit K. Biswas, Oxford University Press, 156-184.

14. April 12, 1997 "Egypt: Back from the Desert" *The Economist*, 36-42.

15. March 5, 1981, World Bank, Report No. 3371-EGT, "Arab Republic of Egypt; Irrigation Subsector Review;" summary, pages i-vi; text pages 1-54; 6 annexes; 3 maps (Drainage Program, Upper and Middle Egypt; Drainage Program, Lower Egypt); 3 schematic diagrams(irrigation systems; drainage systems, Upper and Middle Egypt; drainage systems, Lower Egypt).

16. 1994 "Modernizing Egypt's Irrigation Systems for Sustainable Agriculture" Yehia Abdel Aziz, Proj. Director, Irrig Improvement Project, Cairo; C.A. Hackbart and F.F. Schantz of Morrison Knudsen Corp., San Francisco; Paper No. 94-8015, 17 pages, presented at the June 1994 Summer Meeting of the Am. Soc. of Agric. Engrs.

17. 1996 "Alternative Approaches to Cost Sharing for Water Service to Agriculture in Egypt" C.J. Perry, *Intl. Irrig. Management Institute*, Research Report No. 2, 15 pages.

18. 1985 "Irrigation Projects Review; Supplement to Aide Memoire of July 1985" P.Z. Kirpich in letter of July 30, 1985 to Ulrich Kuffner, World Bank, 9 pages plus time chart..

19. 1988 "National Irrigation Rehabilitation Project; Review of status of Preparation" P.Z. Kirpich in letter of November 2, 1988 to Roy Hewson, World Bank, 4 pages plus two annexes: "Additions to the Terms of Reference of the Consulting Firm" (16 pages); "Possible Assistance from IIMI in the Implementation of NIRP" (4 pages).

20. 1992 "Irrigation Water Management in Sudan" Elsayed Ali. A. Zaki, *op. cit.*, 103-106.in "Country Experiences with Water Resources Management;

Economic, Institutional, Technological and Environmental Issues," World Bank Technical Paper No. 175, 81-92.

21. May 13, 1983 "Gezira Rehabilitation Project; Staff Appraisal Report" Report No. 4218-SU, 90 pages plus 2 maps. "Implementation Volume," consisting of 4 annexes, has 171 pages.

22. July 1987 "Intensification of Irrigated Agriculture in the Sudan and Transmission of Malaria and Bilharzia" K. M. Abdu et al, *ICID Bulletin*, vol.36, no. 2, 24-34.

23. November 2, 1988 "National Irrigation Rehabilitation Project; Review of Status of Preparation," 4 pages plus Annex 1 "Additions to the Terms of Reference of the Consulting Firm" 16 pages; and Annex 2 "Possible Assistance from IIMI [International Irrigation Management Institute] in the implementation of NIRP" 4 pages. Attached to letter of same date to   Roy Hewson of the World Bank.

24. May 1990 "The Gezira Irrigation Scheme in Sudan" Hervé Plusquellec, World Bamk Technical Paper No. 120.

25. March 1980 "Options for Water Resources Control in Jordan" Harold Shipman, World Bank, 19 pages.

26. 1992 "Jordan's Water Resources: Technical Perspective" Radwan Al-Mubarak Al-Weshah, *Water International*, 17 (1992) 124-132.

27. 1995 and 1996 "Sustainable Development of Water Resources and Possible Enhancement Technologies and Application of Water Supply in Jordan" B. Al-Kloub and T.T.Al-Shemmeri, *Water International* 20 (1995) 106-109; "Evaluating Market-Oriented Water Policies in Jordan: A Comparative Study" M. R. Shatanawi and Pdeh Al-Jayousi, *Water International* 20 (1995) 88-97; "Sewage Effluent Reuse in Jordan" S.S.E. Taha and R.F.Stoner, *ICID Journal* (1996) vol. 45, no. 1, 39-57.

28. April 1989 "Technological and Institutional Innovation in Irrigation" World Bank Technical Paper No. 94. David Melamed "Technological Developments: The Israeli Experience," 23-36; Meir Ben-Meir "Establishing Research Priorities," 108-112; Moshe Sne "the Role of Extension in Irrigation," 116-127.

29. October 1952 "Report on the Development of the Tigris and Euphrates River Systems" Knappen-Tippetts-Abbett-McCarthy, Engineers, New York and Baghdad; summary, 10 chapters, 92 maps and charts.

30. 1994 "Problems of International River Management: The Case of the Euphrates" John Kolars, in Waters of the Middle East," Asit K. Biswas, ed., Oxford University Press, 44-94.

31. 1989 Whittleton, C. "Oil and the Iraqi Economy," chapt. 3 in "Sadam's Iraq: Revolution or Reaction?", London: Zed, 54-72.

Chapter 9

STEPS TOWARD EFFECTIVE WATER MANAGEMENT

Planning Perspectives and Check Lists

The goal of effective water management for food production in developing countries can be considered from three perspectives: global, regional and project.

Global Perspective

As described in Chapter 1, there is a general consensus among leading authorities that there is no threat of a global food shortage but that it is urgent to institute planning to avoid shortages in several key regions, all of which are in the developing countries.

Since humanity uses only 54 percent of accessible runoff (Chapter 1), it can be concluded that, globally, there is ample water for all on the planet. The trouble, however, is that water is not distributed uniformly so that many *regions* suffer shortages, some critically. It is therefore preferable to examine water management from the viewpoint of regions or large river basins.

The possible effect of widespread climatic changes resulting largely from burning of fossil fuels, mentioned in Chapter 1, is a global problem about which there is disagreement among scientists, although most feel that advanced long-range planning is needed—from global as well as regional perspectives— in order to be able to cope with possible climatic-induced changes.[i]

Regional Perspective, Issues

A noteworthy examination of regional issues in developing countries, was carried out by the VIIth World Water Congress of the International Water Resources Association, held in Rabat, Morocco in 1993.Twenty-four out of 200 papers that were presented were selected and published in a book.[ii] A summary of the contents of the book, from a published review by the author,[iii] follows.

- All of the papers dwell on the complexity of today's water problems and plead for more coordination and more holistic and multidisciplinary approaches, even when such approaches are difficult owing to contrasting viewpoints, as between environmentalists and developers.
- The reconciliation of these differing viewpoints is particularly urgent in the low-income developing countries. These countries are mainly in tropical or arid zones where water—either too little or too much—is a key problem. One paper states that western thinking may not be appropriate in these countries where water scarcity results in food scarcity, making water-pollution abatement of comparatively lesser importance.
- In sub-Saharan Africa, the high annual loss rate of tropical forests (3.6 million ha or 5.2 percent) and the low proportions of clay and organic matter in African soils, make them particularly susceptible to erosion. Reasons for poor performance of river basin organizations are of an institutional nature or due to lack of political will. This brings to mind a recent reference that makes a strong plea for privately developed small-scale irrigation, supported by agricultural credits from banks and by government-supported infrastructure for electricity and roads.[iv]
- Countering propaganda emanating from some environmentalists against dams, a paper defends the utility of dams for water supply and hydro power, claiming that all that is needed is objective analysis taking into account positive as well as negative benefits. Such an analysis would show that there still remain important sites in the world for dams.

Concerning water planning in Asia, the following major points are made:

- A super project for water transfer from the Brahmaputra River to the Ganges River appears doubtful for the foreseeable future. [Author's note: embanking the Brahmaputra to contain floods, mentioned in Chapter 3, would further complicate such a super project.]
- Groundwater appears favorable in various parts of Asia but need exploration and monitoring to safeguard quality.
- Local banks have important roles for rural development as for small-scale irrigation and village water supplies.
- Remedial works are planned for the severe deterioration of the Aral Sea and surrounding area resulting from over-intensive irrigation.

With respect to water policy the main points are:

- Approaches to planning and implementation must be integral, multisectoral and multidisciplinary.
- Relatively speaking, technological problems are far less difficult to solve than political, institutional and social ones.
- Water planners need to understand better the differences between the situation and needs of water-resource development in western developed countries as opposed to tropical and subtropical underdeveloped countries where (a) quantity rather than quality is presently of greater importance and (b) most of the population is engaged in agriculture but landholdings are very small..
- Serious environmental effects resulting from irrigated agriculture (especially salinization) and from urban pollution (especially contamination of groundwater) need more attention than heretofore.
- Environmental impact assessments often overstate negative effects of development and understate the positive effects, or they fail to consider modifications to development projects that can reduce the negative effects.
- Water pricing, especially for irrigation water, while politically sensitive, has to be introduced more widely. Privatization, best attainable with small-scale projects, can help to achieve adoption of water pricing. Basic infrastructure as for road transport and perhaps electricity, is a prerequisite for which government support is essential.
- ·Water planning needs much more participation by local scientists and development experts, by the population of the local areas to be

developed and by politicians, the latter at both local and national
level.

* ·International agencies have not carried out their roles adequately.
  For example, they have not been forceful enough in insisting on
  covenants regarding water pricing, operation and maintenance, and
  institutional reform. Another example is failure to take initiatives
  toward resolving water conflicts of an international nature.
  [Author's note: See section below: "The Role of the International
  Agencies."]

Regional Perspective, Check List

For ease of reference, the items, in the check list below, are
numbered R1, R2, etc.

R1.Current proposals should be part (a phase) of a long-range plan,
sometimes called a "Master Plan" or a "Framework Plan". The latter
term is preferable as it implies that long-range plans can be modified
and updated as appropriate.

* Master (or Framework) Plans were described in Chapters 3-8 for
  11 cases. Of these, 8 were considered fair to good at the time (may
  need updating) while 3 were considered to be inadequate.
* **Mexico**, with assistance from the World Bank, established a
  National Water Commission—Plan Nacional Hidraulico (PNH).
  PNH completed a "National Water Plan" in 1975 and updated it in
  1980. As described in Chapter 6, economic and political factors
  greatly affect the scope of future water-resource developments.
  Among these are marketing of high-value crops in the United
  States and land-tenure adjustments in the semi-humid Gulf Coast.
* **Tunisia**, fearing imminent water shortages and environmental
  problems, has been taking significant steps for establishment of a
  permanent staff for the planning of regional and country-wide
  water-resource framework plans, but much remains to be done
  (Chapter 4).
* In **Colombia's Upper Cauca Valley**, framework planning, as
  described in Chapter 6, proceeded expeditiously in the 1950s and
  1960s. Local politicians and business men formed a provincial
  corporation, which got no support from the national government
  other than the power to impose a tax on real estate. The tax enabled

the corporation to proceed with planning, with little or no delay before start of actual construction. In its initial phase the emphasis was on electrification province-wide plus two local developments for drainage and flood protection and one for drainage, flood protection and irrigation. The successes in the Upper Cauca Valley entitle it to be held up as a model for similar developments elsewhere.

- India's very large **Narmada Development** (Chapter 3) responds to a pressing need for more food production through irrigation and for more electric energy generation. The central government and the governments of the two States mainly involved—Gujarat and Madhya Pradesh—have pressed ahead despite opposition from neighboring States and from environmentalists, both Indian and foreign. As a result of this opposition, the World Bank decided not to back the project. Planning in the author's opinion was somewhat over-hasty, first because it was done too quickly and second because the projected construction and implementation schedule was unrealistically short, as a result of which the economic and social returns may be materially less than anticipated.

- "Master Plans" for eight regions in **Greece**, prepared in the 1950s, set a pattern of *holistic planning* and also formed the basis for several major projects. Development of three of the regions has since proceeded, but with substantial modifications from the original master plans (Chapter 7).

- **Portugal** in the 1970s had 620,000 ha under irrigation, almost all small-scale by the farmers themselves in the northern coastal and piedmont zones. Some abortive attempts have been made to prepare a national water plan as part of an effort to reverse drops in agricultural production, with focus on the large semi-arid Alentejo region which is promising for intensive livestock, provided supplementary irrigation can be developed to support forage crops during the dry season (Chapter 7).

- **Egypt**, in a race with population growth and loss of arable land to urbanization, has undertaken major water-planning efforts during the past several decades (Chapter 8). These efforts, which certainly must continue, do not suffice. Outside assistance that is already provided will have to be increased, not only as financial aid but also to assist in finding ways to achieve long-term solutions for protection and allocation of the Nile waters among the several countries concerned, especially Ethiopia, Sudan and Egypt.

- **Jordan** has had a water plan that involves strict rationing (Chapter 8) but which is bound to result in much hardship unless ways can be found to increase supply from the Yarmouk, a tributary of the Jordan with a river basin almost entirely within Syria. The only other alternative is the so-called Peace Pipeline from Turkey. However, neither solution seems feasible in the absence of accommodations among the nations concerned, and such accommodations are not likely to occur without strong support from leading world powers, especially the United States.
- In **Bangladesh** master planning has been going on for several decades but with little tangible results (Chapter 3). The country has also suffered from protracted disagreements between those favoring large-scale vs. small-scale works, with the latter winning the argument up to now. In recent years, the realization has grown that a synthesis of the two approaches is what is needed. As in the case of Egypt, much international aid—financial as well as political—will be needed over a sustained period.
- **Ecuador's** Lower Guayas River basin, which contains by far the largest bloc of potentially high-value agricultural land in the country, has been badly mismanaged. The primary problems of the Lower Guayas are drainage and flood control, followed by supplemental irrigation obtained from copious groundwater. Instead, emphasis has been given to large-scale infrastructure for irrigation of the arid Santa Elena Peninsula, for the benefit of a small number of landowners. Hopefully, there has been growing understanding In recent years that the priorities previously assigned were erroneous (Chapter 6).
- **Sudan** has not made adequate use of its share of the Nile waters (Chapter 8). Two main reasons have been failure to carry out effective water-resource planning and political instability caused by the protracted civil war between the northern and southern parts of the country. Once political conditions become sufficiently stabilized, Sudan will need major foreign assistance for rehabilitation of its large existing irrigation perimeters, for long-range planning and for negotiations with the adjacent countries with which it shares the waters of the Nile.

R2. Framework plans should avoid "lumpy investments" and should instead favor gradual, phased investments. There is need to circumvent *monumentalism*, which, besides satisfying an all-too-prevalent desire to build large, impressive structures, offers almost ideal opportunities for corruption.   Although large structures are not always bad, their justification must be made clear in comparison with small-scale developments.

- In **Morocco** (Chapter 4), large dams have served their purpose in some instances but not others. Three large dams built in recent decades in arid zones do not appear justified since they upset the *spate system* previously practiced by peasants.
- In the **Ivory Coast** (Chapter 5), the president's desire for a large dam for hydroelecticity and irrigation—actually a "monument" near his home town— overcame a more rational approach for an alternative development involving thermal power and small-scale, supplementary irrigation in a zone of relatively high rainfall.
- In **Peru** (Chapter 6) a mammoth trans-Andean project has long been promoted for irrigation of a desert in the southern region of the country which would be a poor investment as compared with rehabilitation of existing irrigation projects in the central and northern regions.
- In **India**, the controversial **Narmada Development** (Chapter 3) involves, besides several major dams, a gigantic canal to serve an irrigated area 2 million ha in extent. In the author's opinion, the rate of development planned is too short and should be extended, thus allowing time for evolutionary and flexible adjustments that will surely be needed for so large a scheme.

R3.Planning should be *holistic* meaning that all elements are taken into account including engineering features, economic and financial returns, sociological factors, the environment and special national objectives such as land-tenure reform, food self sufficiency and military security. (The phase currently being planned, while it may not be able to carry out all actions needed to deal finally with all the elements, must at least *consider* them so that the actions can be taken in later phases.) Such an approach was unfortunately not taken in the cases cited in R2.

A key reason for failure to use a holistic approach is lack of leaders of sufficiently broad vision, which may in turn be ascribed, at least in part, to educational deficiencies. For example, engineering education in the United States is overly narrow, with little or no courses in economics and the humanities.[5]

R4.Planning should be *bottom-up* as well as *top-down*, meaning that local desires and interests should be taken into account. In general, bottom-up approaches have almost never been used until now.

- Planning for the **Ganges-Kobadak project in Bangladesh** (Chapter 3) failed to give adequate consideration to the prevailing very small size of landholdings and the need to mobilize local villagers for equitable distribution of water and for operation and maintenance.
- The **Na Xai Thong project in Laos** (Chapter 3) includes a large dam and gravity distribution system ill-suited to the landholding pattern (very small holdings) and humid climate. Groundwater development for *supplementary irrigation* would me far more suitable and would meet the desires of the local farmers..
- In **Mali** (Chapter 5), where large-scale irrigation distribution systems have largely failed, small-scale irrigation based on groundwater appears promising. Local leadership would have to be mobilized and trained, an effort that is essential in any case to deal with the concurrent problems of farm-level planning and marketing of crops and livestock.
- An exception to the foregoing is the **Upper Cauca Valley in Colombia** (Chapter 6) where progressive local business leaders and politicians set up an autonomous, self-financing corporation.

R5.Planning at the top level by various agencies, whether national or regional, should be coordinated, with preferably a single agency in charge.

- The very large **Gezira Project in Sudan** (Chapter 8), 900,000 ha in extent, requires major rehabilitation.. The four separate agencies involved often do not act in a coordinated manner.
- In **Bangladesh** (Chapter 3) rivalry between the Water Development Board, which favors large-scale works, and the Agricultural Development Corporation, which favors small-scale works, has interfered with development.

R6.It may be advantageous to employ local or foreign consultants. There needs to be a procedure whereby the performance of consultants is adequately monitored and evaluated, with conflict of interest avoided.

- In **Mexico** (Chapter 6) foreign consultants were used successfully to prepare a National Water Plan and, just as importantly, to establish a permanent national water commission.
- In the **Upper Cauca Valley of Colombia** (Chapter 6) foreign consulting firms were engaged but with the understanding that a strong local group of planners would be established for further continued planning.
- **Greece** (Chapter 7) made use of a foreign consulting firm that helped set up a pattern for future holistic planning.
- In **Bangladesh** (Chapter 3), foreign consultants failed to take account of fundamental differences in social and economic conditions in Bangladesh as compared with their home countries. Some conflict of interest also took place when consultants recommended large-scale works in the hope of getting additional engagements for design of the works.
- In the **Ivory Coast** (Chapter 5) a similar conflict of interest occurred.

R7.Supporting infrastructure—roads, communications, electricity supply, health and education facilities—should be specified, including what part of these will be included and what part carried out separately but concurrently.

R8.Specify national macro-economic policies that will affect the proposed development, including collection of water charges, land taxes, price supports, subsidies and import/export taxes.

R9.Specify national or regional policies concerning land-tenure reforms. Although much needed, this element has often been lacking or poorly implemented.

- In **Northeastern Brazil** (Chapter 6) extreme inequity in land distribution is a leading cause of social unrest and acts as a brake on growth of agricultural output.
- **Mexico** has extensive areas in the tropical-humid Gulf Coast that are devoted to low-yielding cattle ranches. Land reform, combined with water-resource planning—for drainage and supplemental

irrigation—could substantially raise the agricultural output of this region..

- **Peru's** (Chapter 6)   attempts at land reform were largely unsuccessful. The main reason for the failure was that land was distributed without clear water rights or without supplementary but essential inputs such as farm credit, agricultural extension and marketing support.

R10. Specify requirements regarding farm credit and marketing of agricultural production. Owing to the generally small size of landholdings and low levels of education, these requirements have basic importance for irrigation projects in all developing countries. An important organizational concept in this regard is that of the *water user association (WUA),* with respect to which Non Governmental Organizations (NGOs) have had an increasing role in recent years; see also P6 below and item 3 (User Participation) in Part 1 of the Appendix.

R11 Specify management requirements with respect to staff and client relations. Determine whether a management expert be called in to analyze and make recommendations on items like staff training and incentives, avoidance of corruption and annual reports. (Annual reports, besides providing statistical data, should be tailored to inform and gain support of the general public.) These fields, almost universally neglected, need innovative approaches, as described in a 1987 paper by the author.[6]

R12.   Complex developments in large river basins or regions, which involve major infrastructure and multiple uses of water for purposes other than agriculture, will require sophisticated analysis and mathematical modeling. For such cases, the establishment of a permanent planning group is essential on a continuing basis in order to modify and update the Framework Plan. Foreign experts can provide valuable advice on a part-time basis as for Tunisia (Chapter 4) and for the Narmada River basin planning in India (Chapter 3).

Project Perspective, Check List

P1. Specify the project's objectives including: economic benefits, to the nation and to the individual farmer; financial, to the project and to the individual farmer; other, including equitable income distribution among the landholders, food security and gain in foreign exchange. The financial benefit to the farmer (in terms of the percentage return on his investment in labor and inputs) should be sufficient to ensure his participation in the project; this should normally be from one-and-a-half to twice the interest rate charged for small bank loans.

P2. In calculating the economic benefits, negative benefits, such as environmental damage if any, should be considered. Standard procedures should be used to calculate the economic and financial benefits.[7]

P3. The project's irrigation distribution system should be able to assure that water deliveries to farmers are timely and adequate as to quantity and quality. Use of automatic gates and other, more advanced water-control devices may be useful for the attainment of these goals but should take into account costs, landholding patterns and social factors; see final paragraph in the discussion of the case of Morocco in Chapter 4.

P4. Drainage should be adequate to prevent waterlogging and salinity.

P5. Specify Pilot Zones that will be set up for water-management and crop trials. These were proposed in the Gezira Project in Sudan (Chapter 8) but unfortunately not implemented.

P6. Specify a program for the establishment of Water User Associations (WUAs) similar to what is currently being set up in Egypt and elsewhere.[8] The program should include recruitment and training of local persons to be leaders of the WUAs. See also R10 and item 3 (User Participation) in Part 1 of the Appendix.

P7. Specify how operation and maintenance (O&M) will be carried out and by whom, and how paid. Deficient O&M is a universal problem caused by short-funding (low or non-existing water charges) as in Bangladesh, jurisdictional rivalries as in Sudan, or faulty design, also as in Sudan. Designate the agency or agencies that will carry out O&M and specify what the role of the WUAs will be with respect to O&M.

The Role of the International Agencies

International agencies have an important—sometimes crucial—role to play with respect to food production and water-resource development in developing countries. Some of the international agencies provide technical assistance, some finance and some both technical assistance and finance. Upwards of 50 Non-Governmental Organizations (NGOs) have also assumed important roles in various countries.

Among the leading international agencies are those listed in the box.

The Multilateral Banks

The multilateral banks, like the World Bank, the Asian Development Bank and the InterAmerican Bank, have at times been criticized by environmentalists for alleged damage to the environment or for social costs resulting from forced resettlement of people, when caused by projects that they help to finance.[9] Some of the developing countries also resent what they consider the disproportionate weight of the wealthy countries on the board of direction of the banks.

Other criticisms have concerned the effectiveness of the banks in promoting the *efficiency of irrigation*, defined broadly so as to include, besides water distribution, economic output, equity of distribution and sustainibility.[10] An important tool available to the banks is the use of *covenants* which are agreements attached to loan documents whereby a borrower agrees, as a condition of a loan, to correct prevailing faults such as collection of water charges, faulty maintenance, etc. While making the corrections may be politically painful, it is important that they be carried out in the interest of both the borrower and the lender.

With respect to international water conflicts like that of the Middle East, while as previously noted these are greatly affected by political considerations, the banks can be faulted for failure to take the initiative to alert world political leaders regarding the many ramifications of these conflicts and the need to foster negotiations among the contending parties. The banks could further point out that once sufficient progress has been achieved in the negotiations, they would be in a position to finance a major portion of the investments required.

As the most prestigious agency—and with the greatest financial strength—the World Bank has a *responsibility* to be a leader in

International Organizations Concerned with I&D in Developing Countries

	Finance	Tech. Assistance	Tech. Publications
ADB – Asian Development Bank	•	•	•
ASCE – American Society of Civil Engrs.			•
AGU – American Geophysical Union			•
AWRA – American Water Resources Assn.			•
FAO – Food & Agriculture Org.anisation, UN		•	•
GWP – Global Water Partnership, Stockholm		•	
IADB – Interamerican Development Bank	•	•	•
IBRD – Intl. Bank for Reconstruction and Development (World Bank)	•	•	•
ICID – Intl. Commission in Irrig. & Drainage		•	
IDRC – Intl. Devt. Research Centre, Ottawa	•		
IFAD – Intl. Fund for Agric. Devt., Rome	•		
IFPRI – Intl. Food Policy Research Institute, Washington		•	•
IIMI – Intl. Irrigation Management Institute, Colombo, Sri Lanka (now IWMI)		•	•
ILRI – Intl. Institute For Land Reclamation, Netherlands		•	•
IPTRID – Intl. Program for Technical Research In Irrigation and Drainage, Washington		•	
IWMI – Intl. Water Management Institute, Sri Lanka (see IIMI)			
IWRA – Intl. Water Resources Association			•
MEWIN – Middle East Water Information Network, Philadelphia			•
OAS – Organization of American States		•	
UNDP – United Nations Development Programme		•	
USAID – U.S. Agency for Intl. Development		•	
USCID – U.S. Committee on Irrigation and Drainage			•

resolving or at least mitigating the water crises of the present and of the future. The Bank is in fact well aware of this responsibility as are evident from recent actions and written pronouncements.

Within the Bank, the primary responsibility for water-resources policy rests with the Vice President for Environmentally Sustainable Development, presently (1998) Ismail Serageldin. A recent pamphlet by Serageldin contains a frank discussion of the Bank's past involvement with water-resource developments, describing failures as well as successes.[11] To avoid the "stark and terrible failures" such as have occurred in the past and which were caused by "current water management practices and policies," the pamphlet advocates a new framework for the management of water resources. The blame for principal failures of the past is placed squarely on government mismanagement of water as "the greatest cause of serious misallocation and waste." An article by Serageldin making the same argument appeared about the same time in a leading journal.[12] The principal failures were placed in four groups:

a. Fragmentation of water management among sectors and institutions, with little regard for conflicts or complementarities among social, economic and environmental objectives.

b. Heavy dependence on centralized administration to develop, operate and maintain water systems. The agencies charged with water management are severely overextended and have limited technical capacity to provide quality services. Users are rarely consulted or otherwise involved in planning and managing water resources.

c. Low-value users are allowed to consume large quantities of water without paying for it, forcing high-value users to incur steep costs in securing water from long distances.

d. Environmental degradation of water resources causes human suffering and burdens future generations with the costs of remedial actions.

Two important World Bank publications relating to water resources appeared one or two years earlier. The first, in 1993, dealt with policy of the Bank with respect to water resources[13] and the second, in 1994, reported on a major conference on "Actions to Reduce Hunger Worldwide", hosted by the Bank November 30-December 1, 1993; participants at the conference, from around the world, included political leaders and officials of about fifty Non-Governmental Organizations

(NGOs).[14]   The principal points of these two publications are summarized in Parts 1 and 2 of the Appendix.

Global Water Partnership and World Water Council

Established in August 1996 and with a small secretariat based at Stockholm, the announced intention of GWP is to translate the "Dublin-Rio Principles" for holistic water resources management into operational practice within countries, regions, and collectively on a global basis. To guide its work, GWP has a Technical Advisory Committee (TAC) and a Financial Support Group. Ismail Serageldin, Vice President of the World Bank for Environmentally Sustainable Development, is the chairman of GWP. Proposals for actions to be taken are presently under consideration.[12]

Institutions mentioned as "potential associated programme network partners" included IIMI, FAO (its Water and Sustainable Development Programme), IPTRID and ICID.

Five priority programmes being developed by TAC, representatives of potential partner institutions and the GWP secretariat. are described in Part 3 of the Appendix. The World Water Council, which is based in Marseilles and has existed since 1994, considers itself to be a *think tank* on World Water Policy. WWC maintains contacts with GWP which it regards as a body concentrating on "arranging, funding, and implementation of water development projects."[15]

Conclusions with respect to the international agencies

The two key international agencies concerned are the UN and the World Bank. As a Bank vice president has stated,[16] the Bank has a *comparative advantage* "to deal with institutional development and overall policy and program implementation"—all crucial as this book has repeatedly stated. Cooperation and joint participation with the NGOs are also needed.

1. Strong political support, especially from the United States, will be essential to assure adequate funding for requisite staffing within the UN, the Bank and the GWP, and to exert pressure aimed at resolving major water conflicts that impede development within several major river basins such as the Nile, the Tigris/Euphrates and the Brahmaputra/Ganges. In this connection, part of a

statement by David Beckmann, a former Bank staff member and now head of an NGO *Bread for the World* (see Item 4, Part 2 of the Appendix) is worth repeating: " What happens in the White House will have more impact on world hunger than any decisions here at the World Bank."

2. Placing responsibility on the White House may however be an oversimplification since the attitude of the United States Congress is also crucial. As two seasoned observers have pointed out,[17][18] the Congress has failed to reinstate the Water Resources Council, which had been abolished by President Reagan. With the United States lacking a body to set water-resources policy in a sustained and effective manner within its own territory, it is not in a strong position to influence policy in other countries and in the planet as a whole.

3. Some changes in the Bank's management procedures appear to be called for as regards adherence to covenants with borrowers, coordination with other international agencies and internal staff problems; see items 6, 10 and 11 of Part 1 of the Appendix.

4. Water resource professionals, especially those in the United States, should develop a program to inform the public regarding the crucially serious water situations around the world and why, as a matter of self-interest, the United States must charge the UN and the World Bank to move more swiftly to deal with these situations.

5. Among the eight initial activities for Conserving Water for Agriculture (see Part 3 of the Appendix) are four calling for *"developing best practices"*. The Bank as well as other institutions have a wealth of *past experience* that can be drawn upon. For example, the author in the previous chapters of this book has portrayed many *lessons to be learned* that can be drawn upon, and there are others with long experience that can do the same.

6. With respect to GWP's proposed future actions (see Part 3 of the Appendix), some apparent omissions are:

a) Priorities need to be established including realistic time schedules.

b) There are several key regions of the world (such as the Middle East, India, China, Mexico and Brazil) where water shortages have become critical to the well being of the population of the regions and, therefore to their social and political stability; these regions should receive priority attention.

c) Concurrent actions in related fields need attention including education, especially for women, land reform, and family planning.

d) Two impediments not discussed are corruption and lack of holistic leadership; suggested steps to eliminate or at least mitigate corruption need to be taken seriously.[19]

7. To enable recruitment of a permanent staff of adequate caliber, GWP will need strong support including financing. Whether such support is forthcoming remains to be seen.

Imperatives for Developing Countries

Water-resource planners in developing countries would be well advised to make use of the check lists presented above. Many of the Items on the lists are of a policy nature for which water-resource planners will have to obtain guidance from higher levels of government. Among these are the following (identified by the letter and number in parentheses):

- Inter-agency coordination (R5, P7). Will a particular agency be chosen as leader?
- Supporting infrastructure (R7). What will provided by the government and what by the project and/or development program?
- Local support for (a) planning (R4) and (b) operation and maintenance (P7). To what extent will these be encouraged?
- Selection and training of local leaders (P6, P7). Will funds be available?
- Management and training of staff of the operating agency (P6, P7). What support will be provided by the government?
- Corruption. If a problem, what steps are contemplated to significantly reduce it?
- Subsidies, price supports and import/export taxes (P8). Forecasts are needed in order to make economic and financial analyses (P2).
- Farm credit and marketing (R10). What support will be received?
- Land tenure (R9). What reforms are contemplated? If land is to be distributed, will water rights also be distributed? What land taxes are forecast?
- Increasing planning capability (R3). What training in holistic planning is contemplated?
- Foreign assistance (R6). Should it be sought for technical advice and/or financing? If so, for which of the above?

There is much to do in order to avoid serious water crises, food shortages and social and political instability. The principal players are the developing countries, the agencies of the United Nations, the international banks and the NGOs. Private enterprise has a role but only if the principal players do what is required of them.

A general public that is adequately informed on water-resources issues can provide invaluable support to the principal players. Water-resource professionals have a duty, which is: to generate the needed information program.

Notes

---

1. Nucleus, vol. 20, No. 3, Fall 1998, "Cooking in America—Potential Impacts of Climate Change," Darren Goetz and Elizabeth Farnsworth, 1-3; and "A Small Price to Pay," Warren Leon, 4-5.

2. 1993 "Water for Sustainable Development in the 21st Century" Asit K. Biswas, Mohammed Hellali and Glenn Stout, eds., Oxford University Press.

3. 1995 Review of book "Water for Sustainable Development in the Twenty-first Century" *Water Resources Development,* vol. 11, no. 1, 87-90.

4. May 1990 "Irrigation in Sub-Saharan Africa—The Development of Public and Private Systems" S. Barghouti and G. Le Moigne. Technical Paper No. 123, World Bank.

5. 1989, D.H. Pletta, Distinguished Prof. Emeritus, Virginia Polytech. Inst., discussion of "Developing Countries: High Tech or Innovative Management?" by P.Z. Kirpich, *J. Professional Issues in Engineering,* vol. 115, No. 1, 71-74.

6. 1987 "Developing Countries: High Tech or Innovative Management?" Phillip Z. Kirpich, *J. of Professional Issues in Engineering,* vol. 113, No. 2, 150-166.

7. 1982 "Economic Analysis of Agricultural Projects" J. Price Gittinger, Economic Development Institute of the World Bank.

8. 1997 "User Organizations for Sustainable Water Services" World Bank Technical Paper No. 354.

9. Harald D. Frederiksen "Water Crisis in Developing World: Misconceptions about Solutions" *J. Water Resources Planning and Management*, ASCE, 1996 122(2), 79-87.

10. Water Resources Research (1993). *Special Section: Water Resources Issues and Problems in Developing Countries* American Geophysical Union, Washington, DC 20009, July 1993. Paper #1, D.S. Brookshire and D. Whittington, "Water Resources Issues in the Developing Countries." Paper #2, C.W. Howe and J.A. Dixon, "Inefficiencies in Water Project Design and Operation in the Third World: An Economic Perspective." Paper #3, P. Roger et al, "Water Resources Planning in a Strategic Context: Linking the Water Sector to the National Economy." Paper #4 Eleanor Ostrom, "Design Principles in Long-Enduring Irrigation Institutions." Paper #5, K. William Easter, "Economic Failure Plagues Developing Countries' Public Irrigation: An Assurance Problem."

11. 1995 "Toward Sustainable Management of Water Resources" Ismail Serageldin, World Bank, 33 pages.

12. 1995 "Water Resources Management: A New Policy for a Sustainable Future" Dr. Ismail Serageldin, *Water International 20* 15-21.

13. 1993 "Water Resources Management; A World Bank Policy Paper," 140 pages.

14. 1994 "Overcoming Global Hunger; Proceedings of a Conference on Actions to Reduce Hunger Worldwide" Ismail Serageldin and Pierre Landell-Mills, editors, 243 pages.

15. 1998 Abu-Zeid et al "The World Water Council in Three Years—1994-1997" *Water International* 23 97-106.

16. 1992. Robert Picciotto, Vice President, Corporate Planning and Budgeting, World Bank. "Irrigation in the 1990s: A role for the Bank," in World Bank Technical Paper No. 178,pages 5-7.

17. 1998. Theodore M. Schad, Executive Director of the National Water Commission, 1968-1973. "Water Policy: Who Should Do What?" in *Water Resources Update*, Universities Council on Water Resources, Issue No. 111, Spring 1998, 51-61.

18. 1998. William Whipple, Jr. "Water Resources: A New Era for Coordination," ASCE Press, 123 pages. See final chapter.

19. March 1998 "Fighting Corruption Worldwide" *Finance & Development*. Three articles by Roger Klitgaard, Dean and Distinguished Professor, the RAND Graduate School; Cheryl W. Gray and Daniel Kaufmann, World Bank; Paulo Mauro, IMF.

Appendix

Part 1 - Summary of World Bank 1993 publication "Water Resources Management: A World Bank Policy Paper," 140 pages.

Evaluation of Past Bank-supported Projects

Reviews by the Bank's Operations Evaluation Department showed a sharp drop in recent years. The percentage of irrigation projects rated satisfactory dropped to 44 percent during 1989-90 before rising to 71 percent in 1991, while a decline occurred in water supply and sanitation projects during 1990-91 when 56 percent were satisfactory.

The Bank's New Approach

The Bank and governments have not taken sufficient account of environmental concerns in the management of water resources. The difficulties encountered by Bank-supported projects reflect a large set of problems faced in water resource management, with the situation exacerbated by rapid population growth and urbanization. Costs for new water supplies are much higher than for sources already tapped. New challenges call for a new approach. Three problems in particular need to be addressed:

- Fragmented public investment programming and sector management, that have failed to take account of the interdependence among agencies, jurisdictions, and sectors.
- Excessive reliance on overextended government agencies that have neglected the need for economic pricing, financial accountability,

and user participation and have not provided services effectively to
the poor.
- Public investments and regulations that have neglected water
  quality, health, and environmental concerns.

[Author's note: These three problems are the same as in the two 1995
papers by Vice President Serageldin described above.] As part of this
new approach, the Bank will give priority to countries where water is
scarce and will promote policy reforms, institutional adaptations and
capacity building, *but only when requested to do so.*

User Participation

Water user organizations (WUAs) need to be promoted and made
use of in planning and for operation and maintenance. Field
representatives of the NGOs have been closer to rural villagers than
have Bank staff, are more cognizant of villagers' problems and
capabilities. The Bank will wish to cooperate with the NGOs to a much

Pilot Projects

These are needed to help to introduce new forms of decentralized
management and to refine the design to suit local conditions.

Staff Incentives

Many of the current problems reflect the lack of incentives facing
government entities that provide water services and the consumers' lack
of willingness to pay water charges. [Author: The paper fails to address
incentives to staff for good performance nor the corruption which is
widespread and discourages effective performance by staff.]

Covenants

As the Operations Evaluation Department has pointed out, the
Bank's operational policies and procedures, while basically sound, have
not always been strictly implemented by the Bank, e.g., improper
attention to financial covenants and inadequate cost recovery; lack of
accountability, autonomy, and flexibility in water management;
inadequate investment in sewage treatment and drainage systems;
inadequate concern for poverty relief; neglect of operation and

maintenance; lack of environmental assessments; lack of programs to address erosion problems in upstream watersheds. [Author: Perhaps the Bank could profit from the example of the International Monetary Fund which is often in the position of having to force governments to accept and adopt politically painful but much needed measures.]

Conflicts

The Bank will help countries improve their management of shared international water resources *but only if requested*, presumably by all the governments concerned.

Priorities

Similarly, as with respect to conflicts, the Bank will assist governments in formulating priority policy *if requested*. The Bank will do this through sector work and technical assistance.

Macro-economic measures

Almost nothing is said about subsidies, taxes, price supports and land-tenure reform. A plea by the Bank's president that the Bank "must not be timid" on issues such as land reform was expressed in a recent Bank publication.[1] [These issues, although politically painful, are often of key importance. Perhaps, as stated earlier, the Bank could take its cue from the IMF which generally applies pressure on a government to carry out painful but needed reforms.]

Coordination among international agencies

There is a multiplicity of international agencies, including NGOs, that deal with water-resource problems of the developing countries. How to coordinate these efforts and whether, for specific cases, a single agency should be chosen as leader is not discussed.

World Bank staff problems

Four sets of problems that are not discussed but are important in the author's opinion are:
• Complex water-resource developments require attention on a

continuing basis. The Bank's policy calling for frequent rotation among departments and regions can impede such continuity.

- Promotion policy has tended to favor administrators and generalists rather than seasoned specialists in essential fields including: irrigation and sanitary engineers, agricultural scientists and economists, and development managers.[2] Promotion policy has also tended to favor staff identified with high volume of loans rather than on optimum benefits.
- Recruitment of new professional-level staff has been similarly biased, resulting in an inadequate number of seasoned specialists in the fields mentioned.
- The number of Bank staff assigned to deal with water resources is too low. The Bank is not organized to deal with water globally; whether the Global Water Partnership and the World Water Council (see Chapter 9) can remedy this situation is as yet uncertain.

Placing blame

Placing blame squarely on governments, as was done in the 1998 pamphlet, may be somewhat unfair in view of the faults and/or omissions ascribable to others.

Part 2 - Summary of World Bank 1994 publication "Overcoming Global Hunger—Proceedings of a Conference on Actions" (conference held November 30-December 1, 1993)

1. Poverty, not insufficient food, is the primary reason for hunger in many parts of the world.

2. The concern of the vast majority of participants was to move decisively from rhetoric to action.

3. There were two groups of participants with very different perspectives: One was that of country economic managers, the finance and planning officials who devise countries' macroeconomic and sectoral strategies; the other was that of local nongovernmental and community-based organizations whose staff are in direct contact with poor families.

4. David Beckmann, a former Bank staff member and now head of an NGO *Bread for the World,* made the following points: (a) Staff of the World Bank who are most serious about reducing poverty and hunger are a beleaguered and idealistic minority. (b) NGOs and others who are already working with the poor need to become more political. (c) What happens in the White House will have more impact on world hunger than any decisions here at the World Bank.

5. The Bank's new information policy makes NGO involvement more feasible. What is needed now is a decentralized system of small grants and other assistance to advocacy groups, especially in the developing countries, so that they can modify the pressures on Bank managers and staff as particular decisions are made. [This was excerpted from the same statement by David Beckmann. An additional statement worth noting is by Prof. Robert Chambers of the Institute of Development Studies, Sussex, England, who is highly respected by the NGOs. His criticisms, reflecting prevalent NGO attitudes, were considered pertinent enough to be quoted in a Bank periodical, *Bank's World,* January 23, 1997, item entitled "Shut Up and Listen". Prof. Chambers listed various features of the Bank's *culture* considered objectionable, at least from an NGO point of view. These included rewards for good memos and for bringing projects to the Board while making good presentations to the Board. Penalized behavior included being frank

and honest and giving priority to clients rather than to internal institutional objectives.]

6. Abuses to free trade such as practiced by the United States should stop. An example given: Subsidies to rice farmers averaging $50,000 annually and then using PL 480 rice to keep rice from Guyana from entering the Caribbean market.

7. Hunger is a *population issue*, because, as Lester Brown has noted, the quantity of food in the world is stabilizing, but the curve of population is still going up. Poor nutrition is intimately connected with poor maternal health, high rates of infant mortality, and the disempowerment and illiteracy of women, the very factors that drive up birth rates. [This excerpted from a statement by J. Brian Atwood, Administrator, USAID.]

Part 3 - Proposed Programmes of the Global Water Partnership

Integrated Water Resources Management (IWRM)

Identified gaps are:
- Inadequate awareness of IWRM at all levels of society.
- General lack of mechanisms and tools for the rational allocation, reallocation and reuse of water [no mention of macroeconomic policies to help achieve these goals, nor of measures for poverty elimination, family planning and education].
- Inadequate access to and dissemination of data, information and knowledge. [A Canadian proposal, to help solve and organize in usable form the vast amount of published material, was proposed in 1991.[3]]
- Inadequate institutional framework for cross-sectoral coordination and policy development, including integration of land and water in river basin management.

As a first step, GWP would establish an IWRM Information System in a pilot region, with possible candidates Southern Africa, West Africa and South Asia

A number of donors have expressed interest in supporting IWRM activities under GWP including the German and Dutch governments.

Water Quality Management

Identified gaps are:
- Lack of knowledge of human activities on water quality and of water quality requirements for ecological systems.
- Land conversion with respect to damage to catchments and destruction of wetlands.
- Poor water management: Inefficient use of water, excessive water abstraction and groundwater pumping leading to salinization.
- Pollution by urban and industrial users and by poor farming practices.

The partners involved would include WHO, FAO, UNDP, UNESCO, EDI of the World Bank and several NGOs.

Conserving Water in Agriculture

The capacity for achieving this was found to be weak with respect to:
- Analyzing policies and formulating new policies and legislation.
- Analyzing institutions.
- Setting investment strategies and priorities and mobilizing funds.
- Mobilizing awareness and support for change. Linking with other institutions for integrated water resource management.

There would be eight initial activities, each undertaken by a task force:
- Establish a digital water conservation library and computer programs on the world wide web
- Develop best practices on water saving improvements.
- Develop best practices on rehabilitation strategies.
- Develop best practices on impacts of major managerial reforms.
- Develop best practices on inter-sectoral water transfers.
- Organize high-level policy roundtables.
- Develop and facilitate strategic planning exercise for sets of senior government officials
- Design and stage training courses in policy analysis for consulting firms, planning institutes and donor agencies.

Starting dates for the foregoing tasks would depend on extent of donor interest. The tasks would be carried out over a 3 to 5 year period.

Utility Benchmarking and Performance

The long term objectives would be:
- Enable service providers to design measures to improve their operational performance and provide feedback for the improvement of future investments.
- Provide information to compare performance to that of others.
- Publish data to assist targeting by financing and technical-assistance organizations

The activities would require 18 months to complete to a point where permanent monitoring could be begin.

Urban Environmental Sanitation

At the very time that rapid urbanization is occurring, developing countries are falling behind in providing the needed urban environmental infrastructure and services. The following areas require attention:

- Monitoring indicators for performance benchmarking and post evaluation.
- Private sector participation
- Cost recovery and transparent financing.
- Integrated planning linked to health and environment.
- Consultation and community management.
- Institutional strengthening.
- Appropriate technologies.

Potential partners would include inter alia UNDP-World Bank Water and Sanitation Programme, EDI, UNICEF, USAID. The initial implementation phase would last 3 years. Operations would begin 15 to 18 months after approval of the associated program.

Notes

1. 1997 "Rural Development: From Vision to Action:; a Sector Strategy," World Bank, *Environmentally and Socially Sustainable Development Studies and Monographs Series 13,* pages viii, 18, 91.

2. 1995. Mandivamba Rukuni in " A 2020 Vision for Food, Agriculture and the Environment in Sub-Saharan Africa," IFPRI, Discussion Paper 4, page 49.

3. 1991 "Information Systems for Water Management" Yong-Jo Cho, International Development Research Centre, Ottawa, *Water International,* 16, 214-242.

Glossary

ADC	Agricultural Development Corporation, Bangladesh
ADB	Asian Development Bank, Manila
AGU	American Geophysical Union
ASCE	American Society of Civil Engineers
BWDB	Bangladesh Water Development Board
CADA	Command Area Development Authority, India
CGIAR	Consultative Group for International Agricultural Research
EDI	Economic Development Institute, World Bank
EPWAPDA	East Pakistan, Water & Power Development Authority, Dacca
FAO	Food & Agriculture Organisation, Rome
GNP	Gross national product
GWP	Global Water Partnership, Stockholm
HYV	High yielding variety
I&D	Irrigation and drainage
IBRD	International Bank for Reconstruction and Development (World Bank)
ICID	International Commission for Irrigation and Drainage, New Delhi, India
IDA	International Development Associationn. (affiliate, World Bank)
IFAD	International Fund for Agricultural Development, Rome
IIMI	International Irrigation Management Institute (now IWMI), Colombo, Sri Lanka
IPTRID	Intl. Program for Technology Research in Irrigation and Drainage
ISPAN	Irrigation Support Project for Asia and the Near East (of USAID)

IWMI	International Water Management Institute (formerly IIMI), Colombo, Sri Lanka
IWRA	International Water Rsources Association
KTAM	consultant firm, now "TAMS"
LDC	lesser developed country
NAFTA	North American Free Trade Association
NGO	Non-governmental organization
O&M`	Operation and maintenance
TAMS	consultant firm, formerly KTAM
TIP	Thana Irrigation Plan, Bangladesh
UNDP	United Nations Development Programme
UNEP	United Nations Environmental Program
UNESCO	United Nations Educational., Scientific and Cultural Organisation
USAID	U.S. Agency for Intl. Development
USDA	U.S. Department of Agriculture
WHO	World Health Organisation (of the UN)
WUA	Water user association
WWC	World Water Council, Marseilles

Index

A

B

C

G

Global Water Partnership, 147, 159

Grain
    China, 4
    World production, 3
Greece
    "Master Plans, 137
    Use of consultants, 141

H

Haiti
    Artibonite Plain rehabilitation, 91
    Irrigated agriculture, 91
    Reforestation, 91
High tech. See Morocco, High Tech

I

India
    Indus River, 35
    Irrigated agriculture, 30
    Narmada River development, 33, 137
    System deficiencies, 30
International agencies. See also Bangladesh, Ecuador, India, Ivory Coast,
    Coordination poor, 155
    Global Water Partnership and World Water Institute, 147, 159
    Leadership from developed countries, especially the U.S., 147
    Multilateral banks, 144
    NGOs, 142, 148
    World Bank, 153. See also World Bank
International Water Management Institute (IWMI), 30
Iraq
    Conflicts with Turkey, 127
Irrigation, supplementary, 140
Irrigated agriculture. See also individual countries.
    Regional, 6

About the Author

Phillip Z. Kirpich has had three main careers, all involving water-resource planning and development. The first, with the Corps of Engineers, concerned flood control in mid-Eastern U.S. The second, with a U.S. consulting firm, took him for extended periods to Turkey, Greece and Colombia. The third—and longest career—was with the World Bank. For the Bank, while based in Washington, D.C., he led missions worldwide, with emphasis on South Asia, North Africa, the Middle East and Latin America.

He is a strong believer in *holistic* and *multidisciplinary* approaches, and on the concurrent need to seek and secure local ideas and support. He feels moreover that such support must be sustained through all stages of the development process including planning, construction, operation, maintenance and implementation (which now often includes rehabilitation).

As author of numerous articles in professional journals he has gained international recognition. In 1995 he received the prestigious Royce J. Tipton Award of the American Society of Civil Engineers "For his pioneering contributions to engineering hydrology, his activities in international water-resource planning, and his leadership in development of the National Water Plan of Mexico, the first such national plan in the world."